LOVE NUMBERS

How to Use Numerology to Make Love Count

Margaret Arnold

Gramercy Books
New York

This 2000 edition is published by Gramercy Books™, an imprint of Random House Value Publishing, Inc. 280 Park Avenue, New York, N.Y. 10017 by arrangement with Llewellyn Publications, St. Paul, MN

Gramercy Books™ and design are trademarks of Random House Value Publishing, Inc.

Random House
New York • Toronto • London • Sydney • Auckland
http://www.randomhouse.com/

Printed and bound in the United States of America.

Library of Congress Cataloging-in-Publication Data

Arnold, Margaret, 1952-
    Love numbers / Margaret Arnold.
        p. cm.
    Originally published: 1st ed. St. Paul, Minn. : Llewellyn Publications, 1997.
    Includes bibliographical references.
    ISBN 0-517-16184-2
        1. Numerology. 2. Love—Miscellanea. I. Title.

 BF1623.P9 A675 2000
 133.3'35—dc21

00-026945

8 7 6 5 4 3 2 1

Table of Contents

Part One
Understanding a Name
with Numerology

Part Two
Time in Relationship
to Compatibility

Appendices

Sample Charts of Personal Years

Glossary

Part One

Understanding a Name with Numerology

Introduction

Why do some relationships work and others fail? Why do you almost immediately like some people, but can't figure out why you can't get along with others? Why do you get a feeling of "fitting" with someone, even when it appears by worldly standards that you do not?

These questions and many others can be answered by learning about the interrelationships of energy patterns called vibrations, which make up people's bodies and personalities.

It is believed, as Albert Einstein taught, that everything is composed of energy, and all energy has vibrational patterns. When you learn to understand and analyze these patterns, you also learn the tremendous interworkings among vibrations. One way to learn about vibrations is through numerology, which shows that even the human personality is composed of energy patterns.

Numerology is one branch of metaphysics. Most people think that metaphysics is a lot of nonsense. While there is much useless information in metaphysics, there is also "golden knowledge"—knowledge of extreme value—some of which is the knowledge of the use of vibrations as found in numerology.

The knowledge found in numerology, if known universally, could change humankind. It can teach that there is a place for all, and affirm some of the teachings of the highest souls.

With a knowledge of vibrations, you can know ahead of time how you will interact with other people's personalities or know when to do things to obtain the best results. It is conceivable that deep love and friendship could be available to all. This knowledge can be used to find your mate or find friendship. However, compatibility is an area that covers much more than just love. It has many uses, and many good things could come from this knowledge if it is used correctly.

Knowledge of compatibility can be used in employment situations such as looking for work or putting together a compatible work force. It could also be used to help with adoption. It would be much better to put people together who are actually compatible than to blindly hope that one personality will mesh with another.

Using numerology to look for compatibility could help to know whom to elect to office. One is able to tell what really motivates a person and if it is compatible with what is being sought.

You can use compatibility knowledge in the naming of children. You can create names that are compatible with the people already in the family or that will produce a personality with traits the parents desire for their children. Often, this happens anyhow. As you work with numerology, you will notice that people born within the same family already have vibrational similarities. This shows that souls do not come together by chance. However, this could be consciously used. You could knowingly pick a name that would give your child a personality and interests similar to your own.

You can consciously make love plentiful in your life. Much hurt and hard times could be eliminated.

Wide use of this knowledge is years before its time. However, the fact that it is there, and may someday be widely known, should be heartening to those who have begun to learn the interrelationships of vibrations. Numerology is a priceless body of knowledge. It can be used in many different ways.

What Is Numerology?

As stated before, it is thought that everything is made up of energy. This includes people. Numerology is a means of using numbers to show these energy vibrations. Numerology can be used to show the vibrations of people, the compatibility between them, the vibrations of a time period, or the vibrations of a person within a time period. The numbers, or vibrations, describing a person correspond to one's personality. There are basic traits for each number. The choice is up to the individual whether these traits are lived positively or negatively.

When numerology is used to place a person within time, or to describe a time period itself, the numbers will show the best times to do things. For example, during certain times, love will be heightened. So, if your purpose is to use numerology to look for love or compatibility, it helps to look at the right time, otherwise a chance at love might be lost.

Numerology is said to come from the teaching and calculations of the Greek philosopher Pythagoras, whom most people may remember for the Pythagorean theorem. He was amazingly intelligent and brought great knowledge into the world. It is too bad that his studies and teachings, which led to numerology, are not better known and taken seriously. Numerology could do so much good, but for the most part is not recognized for what it could do.

When using numerology, you learn that certain numbers or vibrations are compatible with others, while other vibrations appear to irritate or repel others. Through much work with the numbers you will begin to see the patterns, balances, and subtle workings of the vibrations. This book will show how to use numerology to recognize compatibility between people. Remember, there are no two people who are 100% compatible. However, in understanding the workings of a relationship, you can create ways to make it better, make it happier, and learn more from the relationship.

This book is not based on any single system of numerology. It comes from years of study and the practical use of a knowledge of vibrations through numerology. It is through this practical use that this knowledge has been proven. This book is one of the very few that teaches people how to use the vibrations that come with time periods. It also introduces the concept of "compound numbers," in which master numbers and the main nine numbers work together.

Numerology and Psychology in Relationships

A knowledge of vibrations explains many things that modern-day psychology cannot. When you work with numerology and vibrations, you begin to notice that in many ways a knowledge of vibrations is really more accurate than psychology. This is because vibrations are energy patterns, and innate vibrations are set at birth. They do not change.

As you work with vibrations to show compatibility, you will find that this knowledge overrides the use of psychology. This means that even if you try to use the best psychology, the vibrations of the situation will always predominate in the end.

If someday the knowledge of vibrations is accepted and widely known, it could help in every type of human relationship. It could save much guesswork in all types of relationships and change the field of psychology.

The Approach to Numerology and How to Use This Book

The approach to numerology found in this book differs from other books. There is no attempt to cover all the areas of the body of knowledge called numerology. Instead, this is a step-by-step guide to using numerology for the sole purpose of being able to judge compatibility between or among people.

Some parts of numerology, which are not needed in the process of determining compatibility, have been left out. New concepts are added to the body of knowledge—some of these new concepts are channeled information or information learned in conjunction with spirit. All the information presented in this book has been used repeatedly by the author and is proven to work. It is invaluable information.

The best way to use this book is to work out the charts step by step. Use the information. Test the information. Use the time charts over a period of time to verify their accuracy. This book attempts to present priceless information in a simple form.

The Value of Knowing the Compatibility Between Names

The value of knowing the compatibility between people is that you can have insight into how relationships between people work. You can get a feel for what is likely to happen within relationships and how to handle what happens. Understanding the people involved and the relationship between them, or between them and yourself, can help work out the relationship. When you understand that people are what their vibrations are, as shown by their numerology numbers, then you have more insight into why people do what they do. From this insight comes tolerance.

To have an idea of compatibility ahead of time makes things easier. It can cut down on time spent "looking for" compatibility by trial and error. It can enhance the depth of love in your life, and the quality of that love. A simple knowledge of numerology will help you accept and understand others better.

Chapter One

Finding the Outer Structure of a Name

To begin to find compatibility between people, as shown by numerology, analyze each name singularly. Letters are converted to numbers to analyze a name. After a name is analyzed by itself, you can continue and learn how the name, or parts of the name, make the person compatible with someone else.

Number Values for Each Letter

Each letter of the alphabet has a value in numerology. These are the basic building blocks in numerology. They range from 1 to 9—except the letter *k*, which has the value of 11, and *v*, which has the value of 22. Use the correspondence chart on the next page to find the value of each letter in the name or names you wish to analyze.

1	2	3	4	5	6	7	8	9
A	B	C	D	E	F	G	H	I
J	K(11)	L	M	N	O	P	Q	R
S	T	U	V(22)	W	X	Y	Z	

Figure 1. *Correspondence Chart: Letters to Vibrations*

Understanding a Name

To begin working with a name, use the chart to figure out the value of each letter in the full name. This is done by matching the letters of the name with their number equivalent, such as is done in the following examples:

```
MARY      JOHN       VALERIE
4 1 9 7   1 6 8 5    22 1 3 5 9 9 5


     KENNETH        LEE
     11 5 5 5 5 2 8   3 5 5
```

Next, the letters are added to find the total value of a name. Addition in numerology is different from regular addition. Before you begin, you should become familiar with the numerology terms defined on the following pages.

Definitions of Types of Numbers

Main Nine Numbers

The numbers 1 through 9 are the main nine numbers—the basic building blocks of numerology.

Master Numbers

Master numbers are numbers made up of the same two digits, such as 11, 22, 33, and 44. These numbers are thought to be stronger or more charged with energy than the main nine numbers. When adding in numerology, master numbers are usually not reduced.

Simple Numbers

Simple numbers are the main nine numbers or the master numbers as they stand alone.

Compound Numbers

Compound numbers are the combination of the main nine numbers and master numbers, or the combination of master numbers with other master numbers. Compound numbers are formed because master numbers are usually not reduced. They are written with commas between the parts of the number to distinguish all the parts of the number.

Lower Vibration

The lower vibration is the equivalent of a master number reduced. Examples of this are:

The lower vibration of 11 is 2.
The lower vibration of 22 is 4.
The lower vibration of 33 is 6.

How Numbers Are Added in Numerology

In numerology, a number is said to equal the digits that make it up.

Example

$$2 = 2$$
$$20 = 2{+}0 = 2$$
$$200 = 2{+}0{+}0 = 2$$

In adding in numerology, the digits that make up the number are added together, over and over, until they cannot be reduced any further. This includes the sums of the digits. The numbers are added and reduced in numerology to find the vibrational equivalent of names or time periods.

Example

$$391 = 3{+}9{+}1 = 13$$
$$13 = 1{+}3 = 4$$
$$3{+}9{+}1 = 4 \text{ (the numerology vibration of 391)}$$

The exception to this general rule is master numbers. Usually, master numbers are not reduced. The only time they are reduced is when it is necessary to see what the numbers would equal if the master number is being lived at its lower vibration. For example, when adding the 11 to other numbers, it is often helpful to add it two ways, both as the 11 and using the lower vibration 2.

Adding master numbers to other numbers creates compound numbers. Compound numbers are created because master numbers are usually not reduced. The concept of compound numbers comes from both the author's applied use of numerology over the course of more than fifteen years and from channeled information. In the past, compound numbers have not been well defined in numerology. Often, the effect of adding master numbers to the main nine numbers has been overlooked or oversimplified by numerologists. However, to produce accurate time and compatibility charts, the concept of compound numbers is important.

A compound number shows both the characteristics of the master number and the main number. Compound numbers are created when master numbers and main nine numbers are joined and are shown by separating the parts with a comma, such as (11,1), (22,6), or (33,8).

To learn how to reduce and calculate numbers, use the practice names provided in the following examples.

Simple Addition in Names

John

$$1+6+8+5 = 20$$
$$20 = 2+0$$
$$2+0 = 2 \qquad \text{John is a 2}$$

William

$$5+9+3+3+9+1+4 = 34$$
$$34 = 3+4$$
$$3+4 = 7 \qquad \text{William is a 7}$$

Kelly

$$11+5+3+3+7 = 11+18$$
$$11+18 = 11+1+8$$
$$11+1+8 = 11+9$$
$$11+9 = 11,9 \qquad \text{Kelly is a 11,9}$$

David

$$4+1+22+9+4 = 22+18$$
$$22+18 = 22+1+8$$
$$22+1+8 = 22+9$$
$$22+9 = 22,9 \qquad \text{David is a 22,9}$$

Adding Main Nine Numbers to Main Nine Numbers

Main nine numbers are added to other main nine numbers like simple arithmetic in order to find their vibrational equivalent.

Example

$$9+5 = 14$$
$$14 = 1+4 = 5$$

Example

$$3+8+2 = 13$$
$$13 = 1+3$$
$$1+3 = 4$$

Adding Main Nine Numbers to Master Numbers

Main nine numbers are added to master numbers by separating the parts of the sum with a comma. If there is more than one main nine number or master number to add, the main nine numbers are added to the other main nine numbers and the master numbers are added to the other master numbers. This forms a compound number, which is written by simply putting a comma between the main nine number and the master number of the total.

Example
$$1+33 = 33,1$$

Example
$$4+1+33+11 = 5+44$$
$$5+44 = 44,5$$

Adding Main Nine Numbers to Compound Numbers

Main numbers are added to compound numbers by adding the main nine number to the main nine number of the compound number.

Example
$$6+11,2 = 11,8$$

Example
$$7+2+22,3 = 22,3$$

Adding Master Numbers to Master Numbers

Master numbers are added to master numbers like simple arithmetic. These can be written as the sum or with commas between the elements.

Example
$$11+44 = 55$$

Example
$$22+33+11 = 66$$

Adding Master Numbers to Compound Numbers

Master numbers are added to compound numbers by adding the master number to the master number of the compound number. The main nine number of the compound number is left alone.

Example

$$22+11,7 = 33,7$$

Example

$$22,3+33 = 55,3$$

Adding Compound Numbers to Compound Numbers

Compound numbers are added to other compound numbers by adding the main nine numbers of the two compounds together, and the master numbers of the compound numbers together.

Example

$$11,3+22,2 = 33,5$$

Example

$$11,4+11,9 = 22,13$$
$$22,13 = 22,(1+3)$$
$$22,(1+3) = 22,4$$

What the Name We Are Reducing Looks Like

Now that you have learned the different types of addition in numerology, use this knowledge to arrive at the numerological value of your names or someone else's using these charts.

First Name

Letters   __ + __ + __ + __ + __ + __ + __

Numbers   __ + __ + __ + __ + __ + __ + __ = __

Middle Name

Letters   __ + __ + __ + __ + __ + __ + __

Numbers   __ + __ + __ + __ + __ + __ + __ = __

Last Name

Letters   __ + __ + __ + __ + __ + __ + __

Numbers   __ + __ + __ + __ + __ + __ + __ = __

Interpretation of the basic numbers in this chart can be found beginning on page 24.

The Expression Number

The final figure in adding up the first, middle, and last name is called the expression number and shows the overall personality of that individual. It is the sum of the total name and comprises the outer structure of a name. To find the expression number, use the whole name as it appears on the birth certificate.

Note: In the case of adoption, use the name given at birth if it is known. The original name will have the strongest vibrations. A name change, such as in adoption, will give some change of vibration, but the strongest vibrations will still be with the original name. In the case of a name that has a descriptor like Senior (Sr.) or Junior (Jr.) following it, find both the vibration with the descriptor and without.

You will find that the personalities produced by the expression numbers have similarities but will also vary—even when the expression number is the same among more than one person. This is because the personality comes from the entire structure of the name, not simply the final expression number.

For example, there are many types of the "3" personality since there are many combinations of numbers that can be a 3 personality. Look at all the following combinations of the 3. The examples on the next page show how varied the makeup of the same expression number can be.

Example: Forms of the 3

$$1+1+1 = 3$$
$$1+2 = 3$$
$$1+2+9 = 3$$
$$1+11 = 1,11 \text{ (a form of three)}$$
$$1+11+9 = 1,11$$

These are just a few of the forms of the three. To get an accurate knowledge of what a personality is like, you must take into account all parts of the name. In the following chapters the interpretation of a name will be broken down further.

Chapter Two

Traits from the Basic Numerology Numbers

In numerology, we have learned that there are different types of numbers. The numbers 1 through 9 are the main, or basic, numbers. The main nine numbers are the building blocks of numerology.

There are also the master numbers and compound numbers. These types of numbers will be explained later in this book, but first, an explanation of the positive and negative qualities of the main nine numbers will be given on the following pages.

The Main Nine Numbers

The 1   The Leader
        The Independent

The number 1 when lived positively gives independence, originality, ambition, drive, force, self-reliance, leadership, creativity, positive willpower, positive egotism, positive dominance, determination, self-assurance, and positive pride. The positive 1 gives the ability to stand alone. It is a number that can make a strong individual.

The number 1 lived negatively gives too much self, negative domineering qualities, too much selfish drive, ambition, willpower, egotism, and pride. The negative 1 may be boastful, conceited, or arrogant. It may make the personality pushy. Impatience or stubbornness might be a problem. The 1 personality might use leadership for self, rather than for the common good. A lack of sharing might be a problem. A very negative 1 could be dictatorial. Basically, the negative 1 becomes too selfish.

The 2   The Follower
        The Gentle

Lived positively, the number 2 gives a cooperative attitude and the willingness to work with others. The positive 2 shows gentleness, receptivity, helpfulness, friendliness, willingness to serve, a loving attitude, consideration for others, sensitivity, the ability to be a good companion, and a striving for harmony. A positive 2 is a good diplomat and might be quiet, contemplative, adaptable, warm, charming, patient, and tactful.

The number 2 lived negatively can give real or perceived over-dependence or the tendency to cling to others. A negative 2 might have nervous problems, and may show instability, vacillation, or a lack of strength to be supportive.

This personality may have problems with shyness, being a doormat for others, being subservient, or being indifferent. The 2 may not have much courage, be oversensitive, and not have a strong physical makeup.

The 3 — The Friendly
Children, Pets and Expression

The number 3, when lived positively, will provide a pleasant outlook on life. A positive 3 will be optimistic, sociable, good-natured, friendly, kind, optimistic, worry-free, talented, and have a joy of living. This personality may have artistic ability and be creative, with a need to somehow express self by some medium. There can be a love of beauty, of children, or a form of self-expression. The positive 3 can have a lot of imagination, be a good speaker, like children or the arts, and have a sense of humor.

The number 3, when lived negatively, may bring jealousy, extravagance, shallowness, and superficiality, as well as self-consciousness and worry. The negative 3 can be a boastful, vain, life-of-the-party type, or a gossiper. This personality may have problems with pessimism and should be careful not to scatter energies. The 3 could try to do too many different things, never master any one thing, and have problems laying a foundation in life.

The 4   The Worker
The "Down to Earth"

The number 4, when lived positively, will give stability, strong foundations in life, a love of work, endurance, conservatism, orderliness, patriotism, and a love of detail. The positive 4 can be very exact and the strong, salt-of-the-earth type. This personality can be economical, practical, and have a great deal of dignity and trustworthiness. The positive 4 can bring security and loyalty. The 4 should use self-discipline.

The negative 4 may exhibit a lack of discipline, loyalty, and honesty. There may be laziness, carelessness, procrastination, conceit, crudeness, narrowness, dullness, rigidity, or sternness. The negative 4 could either hate work or be a workaholic. This personality could be hateful, violent, cruel, resentful, vulgar, or inhumane.

The 5   Freedom Lover
Attractive to the Opposite Sex

The number 5 when lived positively may give a love of freedom, change, adventure, variety, travel, and romance. This personality may seek many different experiences and be very curious and adaptable. There can be an interest in learning and understanding, as well as an interest in sex. The positive 5 is fun-loving and witty.

The negative 5 may abuse personal freedom and not have the ability to commit or be faithful. The negative 5 may fear change, be jealous, inconsistent, irresponsible, undependable, and thoughtless or narrow in thought. Negativity with the 5 might also be seen in an excess of sensuality, sex, or personal freedom.

**The 6   Home and Health
                The Lover of Beauty**

The 6 lived positively makes the personality responsible, loving, friendly, sympathetic, idealistic, understanding, poised, compassionate, firm, stable, and devoted to family. The 6 is a lover of beauty, orderliness, clothes, home, and can be very kind. The positive 6 has the ability to serve, has confidence, and may show a love of music.

The negative 6 can worry too much, be meddlesome, outspoken, unreasonable, domineering, egotistical, or argumentative. There may be problems with jealousy, conceit, cynicism, drudgery, pride, stubbornness, despondency, perfectionism, bluntness, smugness, or domestic tyranny. Anxiety might also be a problem.

**The 7   The Loner
                The Deep Thinker**

The 7 lived positively may have an interest in spirituality or research. The 7 can give the personality a love of studying, knowledge, introspection, quiet, being alone, faith, wisdom, or analysis. The 7 may be a perfectionist and is usually reserved. The positive 7 might be interested in scientific research, writing, or teaching. Meditation or metaphysical topics may be of interest. The 7 may make the personality unusual—a deep seeker or thinker.

Lived negatively, the 7 can give coldness, melancholy, a critical nature, nervousness, confusion, or sarcasm. There may be an aloofness or a dislike of manual labor. The negative 7 can carry the unusualness associated with this vibration too far. This personality may not only have problems being understood by others, but also understanding them. The 7 tends to see things in his or her own way. The 7 is an unusual vibration in that things have to happen by chance. This may be where some of the confusion would come from.

The 8   The Lover of Power
The Lover of Money

Lived positively, the 8 may make a personality desire leadership, authority, or power, and may reflect management or executive ability. The positive 8 is a number of strength, accomplishment, supervision, control, authority, success, strong character, and organization. It is a vibration that can bring much in a material sense. It can also provide courage, self-discipline or self-reliance.

The negative 8 can turn this number's power in the wrong direction. It can bring the lack of material things into a life. It can bring great limitation, strain, hard times, wastefulness, selfishness, and miserliness—or the opposite, a spendthrift. The 8 may be scheming, ruthlessness, hard, intolerant, controlling, abusive, or bullying.

The 9   The Humanitarian
The Teacher

The positive 9 gives a wide outlook on life. It is a vibration that gives a humanitarian spirit and may be very giving and enjoy all types of people. There may be much philanthropy, sympathy, service, generosity, compassion, selflessness, tolerance, understanding, altruism, artistic talent, spiritual-mindedness, or universal love. The 9 also tends to like to teach and to travel.

The 9, if lived negatively, can be selfish—the opposite of the positive 9. The negative 9 might also be immoral, unkind, unstable, nervous, indiscreet, impractical, over-emotional, or bitter. This personality may be unethical, sullen, or vulgar.

The Master Numbers

Some numbers are called master numbers and are thought to be stronger and charged with more energy than the main nine numbers. The master numbers usually considered are 11 and 22, and sometimes 33. Besides these numbers are the 44 and greater numbers following the same pattern. These generally come from adding smaller master numbers, although there are a few names that add up to 44 themselves. Occasionally, a name may add up to a higher master number than 44.

In general, the characteristics of master numbers are intensified traits of the main nine numbers that they add up to, as well as the characteristics of the double number within them. For example, the 33 has the traits of the 3 and the traits of 3+3, or 6.

Also within the vibrations of each master number is the element of the 11. When analyzing the compatibility or characteristics of any master number, all these possibilities should be taken into account.

Usually, only the 11 and 22 are explained in depth in the study of numerology. However, here we will also explain 33 and 44, because some names add up to these numbers. An example of this is the very common name Robert, which is a 33.

For names that add up to a master number higher than 44, the characteristics of the name will be found in both what the name adds up to and those of the double digit within the master number. Look at both the negative and positive characteristics of all the elements.

The 11   Things of God
The Giver

The 11, when lived positively, can give spirituality, extra intelligence, heightened intuition, a willingness to serve humanity, and extra awareness. The 11 tends to be idealistic—a perfectionist and a dreamer. The 11 also brings inspiration. It is called the "God force" number, and under this number it is said that the personality must not be selfish, because the consequences for being selfish under this number are much greater than under other numbers. The 11 can be put in the limelight. An inventive or religious nature is a trait of the 11, and this personality will often lead within the church or within social service work. An 11 personality may also be found in the stage professions or dealing with electricity.

The negative 11 can be very selfish, as it has within it the elements of a double 1. This is something personalities with the 11 should guard against because of the "God force" element associated with the number. Lived negatively, the 11 can give a superiority complex, dishonesty, fanaticism, miserliness, meanness, shyness, over-sensitivity, cowardliness, or a doormat personality. Check the negative characteristics of the 2 to understand more about the negative 11.

The 22   **The Master Builder**
             The Lover of Groups

The positive 22 is the master builder who likes to build for humanity and takes ideals and puts them into a concrete form. The positive 22 is a manager and director, practical and universal. This personality is a lot like the positive 9 in that it likes all types of people. The positive 22 likes groups and likes to work, but particularly in a field seen as having a high purpose. Individuals with a 22 are usually honest, idealistic high achievers. This number may bring an interest in governmental affairs.

The negative 22 can be an intensified negative 4. Check the negative aspects of the 4 to understand possible negative traits of the 22. The negative 22 can have an inferiority complex, begrudge service to others, be very hateful, could be violent. Anxiety may be a problem. Mental disturbances are sometimes associated with the very negative 22—but considering that these can be organic, and many other numbers fall into this category, that possibility is probably very rare.

The 33   **Very Friendly**
             Children, Pets and Expression

The positive 33 is very loving, positive, and confident. The positive 33 loves children and family. This vibration can make the personality a very good speaker or a humanitarian. The 33 will cause a seeking for perfection and beauty. The positive 33 can be successful in many areas, including leading groups in any area demanding good oratory skills, working with children, dealing with domestic activity, or professions with domestic interests.

The negative 33 can be very difficult. This personality may like to argue, and with the added confidence of the intensified 6, the 33 may be quite a fighter. The negative 33 can consider him or herself always right, with little bending for the viewpoint of others. The negative 33 may seek too much perfection, making it hard on self and on others.

The 44   The Hard Worker
The Power Lover

The positive 44 is very strong. It is a form of the eight making it capable of doing a lot of work and being able to handle authority. This personality can have a very strong will and a natural air of authority.

The natural authority at times will come through, but the 4 is a limiting number and will probably tone down this authority. There are not many English language names that add up to 44—Gretchen and Marjorie are examples.

The negative 44 can be very negative. The negative 44 has the element of an intensified 4—and when negative, the 4 can bring hate and restriction. Coupled with the element of the 8, which can be very stubborn, a negative 44 can be very destructive.

Chapter Three

Finding the Inner Structure of a Name

The next step in using numerology to determine compatibility is to find the inner structure of a name. This inner structure is composed of the soul urge and the inner self. We will begin with finding the soul urge.

The Soul Urge

Names can be broken down much further than the expression number used in Chapter 2. Adding together the vowels in a name and reducing that sum to a single digit provides the soul urge. The soul urge is what motivates a person or signifies what a person seeks within his or her heart. It is truly the person's heart's desire.

In reading about numerology, the name numerologists give to this number may differ. Some call it the soul urge, some the heart's desire, and some the secret ambition. Whatever name is used, the meaning and evaluation of this number are the same.

The soul urge is of great importance in assessing compatibility. This is because the soul urge is what is within the heart of the person and shows the characteristics that the person will really have. The importance of discovering what people are "within their hearts" cannot be emphasized enough when you are assessing compatibility. It will save many disappointments.

The Vowels

The vowels used in numerology are the same as those in regular use in the English language: a, e, i, o, u and sometimes y. If there is no other vowel in a syllable of a name, then use y as the vowel. Sometimes, a little knowledge of the person will also help in telling how they should be used.

The Value of Knowing the Soul Urge

The value of knowing the soul urge in analyzing compatibility is that the inner self of each person can be seen. Two people whose compatibility you are analyzing may have conflicting things that motivate them, and this can be seen in the soul urge. For example, a person with an 8 soul urge may conflict with a person with an 11 soul urge because the 8 is very material, whereas the 11 is usually spiritual. This does not mean that two such people could not get along, but it does show where potential conflict might occur. In this example, it might be wise to remember that sometimes those who think materially need those who think spiritually, and those who think spiritually need those who think materially. Be careful not to judge anyone as good or bad, right or wrong. It is best to take the attitude of using numerology to understand differing personalities, not to judge their value. Each soul has its own reason for taking its specific personality.

In looking at the soul urge from the point of view of compatibility, it is wise to think in terms of what the need of compatibility is for. There is a difference between looking at compatibility between potential marriage partners, between employers and employees, and between friends. The use of the compatibility study must be taken into account.

Knowing the soul urge can help people achieve their goals. In looking at compatibility, one should consider if the goals of the others they are seeking to be compatible with are something with which they want to be compatible. Are the goals of the other person something that you wish to help with?

How the Soul Urge Is Charted
In this section, some samples of how the soul urge is charted will be given and a chart for comparing names will be shown. Following that, explanations of what each number means as a soul urge are provided

Example

Mary Elizabeth Smith

First Name   M + A + R + Y

Vowels: A + Y = 1 + 7

                    1 + 7 = 8

Middle Name: E + L + I + Z +A + B + E + T + H
Vowels: E + I + A + E = 5+9+1+5

$$5+9+1+5 = 20$$
$$20 = 2+0$$
$$2+0 = 2$$

The soul urge for the middle name is 2.

Last Name: S + M + I + T + H
Vowels: I = 9

The soul urge for the last name is 9.

The soul urge for the entire name Mary Elizabeth Smith is the sum of the soul urges for each name.

$$8+2+9 = 19$$
$$19 = 1+9$$
$$1+9 = 1$$

The final soul urge for this name is 1.

Comparing the Compatibility of Soul Urges

Use the following charts to determine the soul urges of two people for whom you wish to do a compatibility study.

First Name

Letters   __ + __ + __ + __ + __ + __ + __

Vowels   __ + __ + __ + __ + __ + __ + __

Soul Urge   ____ = ____   ____ = ____

Middle Name

Letters   __ + __ + __ + __ + __ + __ + __

Vowels   __ + __ + __ + __ + __ + __ + __

Soul Urge   ____ = ____   ____ = ____

Last Name

Letters   __ + __ + __ + __ + __ + __ + __

Vowels   __ + __ + __ + __ + __ + __ + __

Soul Urge   ____ = ____   ____ = ____

Next, the soul urges from all the names are added together.

First ____ +   Middle ____ +   Last ____ = ____

The soul urge for this name is ____.

The Soul Urge of the Second Name

First Name

Letters   __ + __ + __ + __ + __ + __ + __

Vowels   __ + __ + __ + __ + __ + __ + __

Soul Urge   ____ = ____   ____ = ____

Middle Name

Letters   __ + __ + __ + __ + __ + __ + __

Vowels   __ + __ + __ + __ + __ + __ + __

Soul Urge   ____ = ____   ____ = ____

Last Name

Letters   __ + __ + __ + __ + __ + __ + __

Vowels   __ + __ + __ + __ + __ + __ + __

Soul Urge   ____ = ____   ____ = ____

Next, the soul urges from all the names are added together.

First ____ +   Middle ____ +   Last ____ = ____

The soul urge for this name is ____

Finally, the full soul urge of each name is compared to the other.

Name A ____   Name B ____

Use the descriptions in the next set of lists to compare the two soul urges.

Characteristics of the Soul Urges

The Soul Urge 1

This person may have the following characteristics.

- likes to be independent
- likes to be a leader
- likes to stand alone
- likes to be alone
- wants to be listened to
- likes to be the boss, or one's own boss
- can be creative
- can be a pioneer and likes to explore things
- can be an initiator
- may be selfish
- might be arrogant
- might lack patience
- might be blunt and lack tact
- likes to create opportunities for others to praise him or her

The Soul Urge 2

This person may have the following characteristics.

- likes to follow, rather than lead
- is very sensitive
- likes to be with others
- can be diplomatic
- can be gentle

- has to be careful not to give to the detriment of self
- likes a peaceful environment
- seeks harmony with others
- has to be careful not to be a doormat
- probably will not be a good disciplinarian
- likes those of the opposite sex
- may be psychic, look at the overall numbers to determine this

The Soul Urge 3

This person may have the following characteristics.

- can have much love of life
- usually wants to express oneself in some way
- likes children and animals, might want pets
- likes having friends and socializing, likes parties
- might like speaking or acting, wants to be heard
- might be artistic
- usually is the one to uplift the spirits of others
- has a good sense of humor
- may have a tendency to scatter their many talents
- strives for joy and happiness

The Soul Urge 4

This person may have the following characteristics.

- if positive, will have a love of work
- will be a "salt-of-the-earth" type
- likes order and logic

- is loyal and patriotic
- is very practical
- is conscientious and determined
- can do detailed work, is methodical
- can be stern and harsh
- likes material things
- may have mechanical ability or be able to work with hands
- wants to build a permanent foundation in life
- may be narrow-minded
- is usually a good disciplinarian
- if negative, can harbor hate

The Soul Urge 5

This person may have the following characteristics.

- is a freedom lover
- likes to travel
- does not like details
- has problems sticking to a routine
- may have problems being on time
- naturally attracts the opposite sex, is magnetic
- usually has a high interest in sex
- likes adventure and excitement
- likes change and new interests
- should be careful not to seek change, just for change itself
- likes parties

- has talent with visual skills such as art
- needs to guard against excess in alcohol, gambling, and sex
- may not be a good money manager
- may be intellectual
- is physically oriented

The Soul Urge 6

This person may have the following characteristics.

- has a love of home and family
- has natural healing ability, good in the health professions
- can be very loving
- can handle a lot of responsibility
- likes to argue, but does not want anyone to go away hurt
- is very conscious of what things look like
- wants beauty, comfort, peace and harmony, might be artistic
- likes music and can be musical, may have a good singing voice
- likes neatness
- has much interest in clothes
- has much confidence
- likes to work with others
- likes to do things that are domestic
- likes quality

- may be a comforter and peacemaker for others
- may be a good speaker

The Soul Urge 7

This person may have the following characteristics.

- is a seeker of wisdom and knowledge
- is introspective, likes to be alone, may like to live alone
- might like to meditate and contemplate
- might be religious, spiritual or philosophical
- may be scientific, might be analytical
- is interested in the mysteries of life
- is a deep thinker
- is a seeker of truth
- would like a quiet environment
- may be a perfectionist
- may be interested in metaphysics
- may love nature and the outdoors
- may want to teach
- sometimes very misunderstood by others
- tends to see things in their own way
- needs to cultivate faith
- does not like manual labor

The Soul Urge 8

This person may have the following characteristics.

- wants to do everything in a big way
- is materially oriented
- has managerial or executive ability
- can be very stubborn
- can be good in business, may want to run their own business
- likes to be important, an authority, the leader or boss
- likes large accumulations of money
- has good judgment
- may desire government work
- may like to work with money
- may have good planning ability
- can handle a large amount of work
- can be analytical
- is efficient
- admires power and seeks it
- has courage and strength, can be forceful
- if positive, may have a lot of willpower

The Soul Urge 9

This person may have the following characteristics.

- is a humanitarian
- can be a philanthropist, a real giver
- likes people of all types, is a universalist

- loves to travel
- likes to teach
- does not want to be "cooped up" or "fenced in"
- wants to help mankind
- may be overly generous
- usually very kind; if negative, it is the exact opposite
- has much healing ability, would be good in health professions
- can see the good in everyone
- is willing to serve
- is compassionate
- likes music and the arts
- likes to be independent
- needs to be needed

Master Numbers as Soul Urges

The Soul Urge 11
This person may have the following characteristics.

- can bring inspiration to others
- is intuitive
- should have some way to give in life
- usually will share
- may have an interest in religion or spiritual things
- may have psychic ability
- may be too generous
- may like the limelight

- may deal with aviation, electricity, or the theater
- may want to explore the deeper things in life
- can have high ideals
- may be interested in the metaphysical
- may not be able to live up to the 11, see the 2

The Soul Urge 22

This person may have the following characteristics.

- wants to build on the material plane for the good of all
- can handle a lot of work
- is a universalist and likes all kinds of people
- is a humanitarian
- can lack confidence
- may be domineering
- can have the characteristics of the 4
- may be materialistic, may like to collect or store things
- may be harsh or stern
- is practical
- has high ideals
- wants to do things on a large scale
- likes to be with groups

The Soul Urge 33

This person may have the following characteristics.

- very much likes home and family
- much healing ability and could be very good in healing professions
- can be very loving
- can reach out to humanity
- is able to handle a lot of responsibility
- can be argumentative, but usually does not like to hurt others
- a lover of beauty, comfort and peace
- may be good in artistic endeavors
- is very conscious of appearance of people and things
- can be very neat
- very confident
- likes music and can be very musically talented
- very domestic
- likes to be with others
- likes very high quality
- has good speaking ability
- likes to bring comfort to others
- see the 6

The Soul Urge 44

This person may have the following characteristics.

- usually a very good worker
- likes power and authority

- likes to do things in a big way
- may be a manager or executive
- very material
- very strong personality
- can be a narrow thinker
- very strong willed
- much courage
- can be very stubborn
- is business oriented
- likes leadership and to be the boss
- likes to deal with money
- likes large accumulations of money
- very down to earth
- if negative, can be very negative
- analytical and efficient

The higher master numbers are not often found as soul urges, though they do show up sometimes. Compound numbers as soul urges are more common. When a compound number is the soul urge, check the characteristics of each part of the number as well as the overall vibration to get a view of what the soul urge is like. If a higher master number than 44 is found, go back and read the explanations for all the elements of that number to see what the characteristics are.

The Inner Self

You may find many different names and explanations for the part of the personality that is called the inner self, which is found by finding the numerology sum of the consonants in the name. It is often called by other names such as the quiet self or the latent self. It is thought that this is the part of the personality that lies latent until it is needed, at which time it comes forward. Even though it may be called the inner self, this part of the personality often becomes an outer self, since it is used to accomplish goals. It is often seen by others as it manifests to accomplish goals. It is thought to be a part of the personality used to try to obtain the soul urge and the part that is shown to the world.

The Value of Knowing the Inner Self

It is important to know the number value of the inner self because this is the part of the personality that is shown to others. It is one of the main parts of what a person will be and will appear to be.

The inner self can be compared to the soul urge—what a person is in his or her heart. This comparison gives a more accurate assessment of what the person really is.

This section shows how to chart the inner self. Remember, the inner self is found by adding the consonants in a name. It is the part of the personality that others see and is often different from what a person is in his or her heart.

How the Inner Self Is Charted

In this section, some samples of how the inner self is charted will be given. Charts for comparing names will also be shown.

Example

Mary Elizabeth Smith.

First Name   M +A + R + Y

Consonants   M + R = 4+9

$$4+9 = 13$$
$$13 = 1+3$$
$$1+3 = 4$$

The inner self for the first name is 4.

Middle Name   E + L + I + Z + A + B + E + T + H

Consonants   L + Z + B + T + H = 3+8+2+2+8

$$3+8+2+2+8 = 23$$
$$23 = 2+3$$
$$2+3 = 5$$

The inner self for the middle name is 5.

Last Name   S +M + I + T + H

Consonants   S+M+T+H = 1+4+2+8

$$1+4+2+8 = 15$$
$$15 = 1+5$$
$$1+5 = 6$$

The inner self for the last name is 6.

The inner self for the name Mary Elizabeth Smith is 4+5+6.

$$4+5+6 = 15$$
$$15 = 1+5$$
$$1+5 = 6$$

The final inner self for this name is 6.

Comparing the Compatibility
of Inner Selves

Use these two charts to determine and compare the inner self of those for whom you wish to do a sompatibility study.

First Name

Letters   __ + __ + __ + __ + __ + __ + __

Consonants __ + __ + __ + __ + __ + __ + __

Inner Self   ____ = ____   ____ = ____

Middle Name

Letters   __ + __ + __ + __ + __ + __ + __

Consonants __ + __ + __ + __ + __ + __ + __

Inner Self   ____ = ____   ____ = ____

Last Name

Letters   __ + __ + __ + __ + __ + __ + __

Consonants __ + __ + __ + __ + __ + __ + __

Inner Self   ____ = ____   ____ = ____

Next, the inner selves from the names are added together.

First ____ +   Middle ____ +   Last ____ = ____

The inner self for this name is ____.

The Inner Self of the Second Name

First Name

Letters   __ + __ + __ + __ + __ + __ + __

Consonants   __ + __ + __ + __ + __ + __ + __

Inner Self   ____ = ____   ____ = ____

Middle Name

Letters   __ + __ + __ + __ + __ + __ + __

Consonants   __ + __ + __ + __ + __ + __ + __

Inner Self   ____ = ____   ____ = ____

Last Name

Letters   __ + __ + __ + __ + __ + __ + __

Consonants   __ + __ + __ + __ + __ + __ + __

Inner Self   ____ = ____   ____ = ____

Next, the inner selves from the names are added together.

First ____ +   Middle ____ +   Last ____ = ____

The inner self for this name is ____.

Finally, the full inner self of each name is compared to the other.

First Name ____   Second Name ____

Use the descriptions in the next set of lists to compare the two inner selves. Remember that this is how the person may appear to others.

Characteristics of the Inner Selves

The Inner Self 1

This person may have the following characteristics.

- usually a leader in some form
- dominant
- independent
- wants to be the boss or in control
- an initiator
- arrogant at times
- lacks patience at times
- selfish at times
- has courage to explore and try new things
- egotistical at times
- may appear to push to be heard at times
- pushy in other ways, as well
- may appear to set up situations where he or she will be praised

The Inner Self 2

This person may have the following characteristics.

- may appear to be gentle
- seems to be a follower
- may appear to be sensitive and kind
- may appear to be a joiner, likes to be with others
- the 2 will give a softening of the entire personality
- likes quiet, peace, and diplomacy

- may give too much
- doormat, if too gentle
- appears to like the opposite sex
- seems to be cooperative
- psychic
- may seem to want to be in the background
- may appear to put much importance on family and home

The Inner Self 3
This person may have the following characteristics.

- creative
- appears to want self-expression in some form
- seems to love life
- seems to like to socialize
- this number will uplift the rest of the numbers
- likes to talk
- joyous and happy
- may seem to try to do too much, scattering talents
- likes animals
- likes children

The Inner Self 4
This person may have the following characteristics.

- may appear to love to work
- seems to be orderly, able to handle details
- can appear stern and harsh

- practical
- likes tried and true values
- may appear to be narrow or holding back from joyous expression
- may appear to be determined
- likes material things
- appears to be loyal and patriotic
- if negative, can be hateful

The Inner Self 5

This person may have the following characteristics.

- freedom lover
- likes to travel
- has problems following a routine
- does not seem to like details
- seems to have problems being punctual
- seems to have a natural magnetism and likes the opposite sex
- appears to have a high interest in sex
- likes adventure and excitement
- likes change and new interests
- likes parties
- appears to have talent with visual skills, may be artistic
- problems with excesses of sex, alcohol, or gambling
- problems managing money
- can appear to be intellectual
- seems to be physically oriented

The Inner Self 6

This person may have the following characteristics.

- love of home and family
- natural healing ability, may be in the health professions
- seems very loving
- appears to be able to handle a lot of responsibility
- likes to argue, but does not want to hurt anyone with it
- very conscious of what things look like
- likes beauty, comfort and peace
- may be artistic
- appears to like music and may be musical
- good singing voice
- seems to like neatness
- much interest in clothes
- seems to have a lot of confidence
- appears to like to work with others
- likes to do domestic things
- seems to like quality
- seems to be a peacemaker and comforter of others

The Inner Self 7

This person may have the following characteristics.

- appears to be a seeker of wisdom and knowledge
- introspective
- seems to like to be alone and possibly, to live alone
- appears to be religious, spiritual, or philosophical
- scientific and analytical
- seems to be interested in the mysteries of life
- a deep thinker and a seeker of truth
- likes a quiet environment
- perfectionist
- interested in metaphysics
- appears to like nature and the outdoors
- wants to teach
- seems to see things in their own way
- shows a dislike of manual labor
- seems to be hard to understand

The Inner Self 8

This person may have the following characteristics.

- appears to do whatever they do in a big way
- materially oriented
- appears to have managerial or executive ability
- can be stubborn
- shows a talent for business, may be self-employed
- seems to want to be important, an authority, a leader or boss

- likes large accumulations of money
- appears to have good judgment
- may desire government work
- may like work with money
- seems to have good planning ability
- appears to be able to handle a large amount of work
- analytical
- efficient
- seeks and admires power
- has courage and strength, can be forceful
- seems to have a lot of willpower, or it can be the opposite

The Inner Self 9

This person may have the following characteristics.

- humanitarian
- philanthropist, a giver
- seems to like to travel
- shows a desire to teach
- shows a dislike of being "cooped up" or "fenced in"
- desire to help humankind
- seems to be overly generous
- shows much kindness, if positive; the opposite, if negative
- has much healing ability, would be good in health professions
- appears to like all types of people

- able to see the good in everyone
- shows a willingness to serve
- shows compassion
- seems to like music and the arts
- appears to like to be independent
- shows a need to be needed

Master Numbers as Inner Selves

The Inner Self 11

This person may have the following characteristics.

- seems to bring inspiration to others
- intuitive
- shows willingness to share
- shows an interest in religion or spiritual pursuits
- psychic ability
- too generous
- seems to like the limelight
- may show an interest in aviation, electricity, or the theater
- may show a desire to explore the deeper things in life
- appears to have high ideals
- may show an interest in the metaphysical

The Inner Self 22

This person may have the following characteristics.

- wants to build on the material plane for the good of all
- has the ability to handle a lot of work
- seems to be a universalist and to like all kinds of people
- shows humanitarian qualities
- can appear to lack confidence
- may be domineering
- likes material things
- may appear to like to collect or store things
- may appear harsh or stern at times
- practical
- shows high ideals
- seems to like to do things on a large scale
- seems to like groups

The Inner Self 33

This person may have the following characteristics.

- has a great love of home and family
- has much natural ability to heal
- appears to be good in the health professions
- seems to be very loving
- likes to argue, but not to hurt others with it
- seems to be able to handle a lot of responsibility
- seeker of comfort

- beauty or how things appear is important
- likes music and may be musical
- very neat in appearance and surroundings
- thinks clothing and fashion are important
- may have singing talent
- likes domestic things
- appears to have much confidence
- speaking ability
- seems to bring comfort to others
- seeks high quality
- seems to like to work with others

The Inner Self 44

This person may have the following characteristics.

- very materially oriented
- can be a very good worker
- can be quite stubborn
- may have good managerial ability
- seems to admire power and seeks it
- may appear to be harsh at times
- can have a lot of willpower
- strong personality
- seems to have a lot of courage and force of personality
- may show extreme anger
- seems to like large accumulations of money
- may have business talent

- may be analytical
- may seek to be an authority or boss, but the 4 may hold the person back
- seems to be down to earth
- seems to show good judgment
- may seem to dominate others

After the soul urge and inner self are found, the next step is to put them together. This is done to study the entire inner structure of the name. The following chart can be used to combine the soul urge and inner self.

Soul Urge and Inner Self Combined: Looking at the Inner Structure of a Name

First Name

Inner Self: __ + __ + __ + __ + __ + __ + __ = ____

(consonants) __ + __ + __ + __ + __ + __ + __ = ____

Soul Urge: __ + __ + __ + __ + __ + __ + __ = ____

(vowels)   __ + __ + __ + __ + __ + __ + __ = ____

Middle Name

Inner Self: __ + __ + __ + __ + __ + __ + __ = ____

(consonants) __ + __ + __ + __ + __ + __ + __ = ____

Soul Urge: __ + __ + __ + __ + __ + __ + __ = ____

(vowels)   __ + __ + __ + __ + __ + __ + __ = ____

Last Name

Inner Self: __ + __ + __ + __ + __ + __ + __ = ____

(consonants) __ + __ + __ + __ + __ + __ + __ = ____

Soul Urge: __ + __ + __ + __ + __ + __ + __ = ____

(vowels)   __ + __ + __ + __ + __ + __ + __ = ____

Next, the full inner self from all the names are added together. Then, the same is done with the soul urges.

Inner Self

First _____ +   Middle_____ +   Last_____ = _____

The inner self for this name is _____.

Soul Urge

First _____ +   Middle_____ +   Last_____ = _____

The soul urge for this name is _____.

Inner Self   _____

Soul Urge   _____

Chapter Four

Traits of Compound Numerology Numbers

When working to find the numerology equivalent of a full name, often one of the parts of a name will equal a master number. Some examples of this are as follows.

Angela = 22	Andrew = 11
Ann = 11	David = 22,9
Catherine = 11	Kevin = 22,11,1
Karen = 11,2	Michael = 33
Marjorie = 44	Steven = 22,9
Margaret = 11	Thomas = 22
Susan = 11	Robert = 33

There are many such names. Any name that has a "k" or a "v" in it will be either a compound number or a master number. For that reason, in this chapter, traits of individuals whose names result in compound numbers are listed.

Like master numbers, compound numbers change the characteristics of a personality. A compound number occurs when a master number is combined with one of the main nine numbers. This is when master numbers and main nine numbers appear together. The master numbers are usually not reduced when added to the main nine numbers, however the characteristics of what their sum would be, and what the compound numbers would be if they stood alone, are found in the personality. The following descriptions tell the basic characteristics of each compound number and advise which other numbers can be studied for further insight.

Simple Compound Numbers of 11

The 11,1

Also read the 11, the 1, and the 3.

The 11,1 is a form of the 3, so it has the characteristics of the 3 as well as the 11 and the 1. The 11,1 has the element of leadership, both spiritual and material. It is a compound number where balance is needed between self-interest and the interest of others. A personality with this compound vibration could lead in many ways. Some of the typical places the leadership qualities of the 11,1 can be found include spirituality, science, religion, electronics, the performing arts, social work, or library work. This vibration can help the personality lead in dealing with children, as well.

This vibration will help within the world in a kinder, gentler way than a 1 not accompanied with the 11. The 11 changes the usual self-centered characteristic of the 1.

Look at the overall name very closely to get an idea of the personality involved. The 11,1 can be very intelligent. Also, look at what numbers are forming the 1, as there are many forms of the one. For example, a 1 formed from the addition of a 2 and 8 is very different from a 1 from 1 and 9.

The 11,2

Also read the 11, the 2, and the 4.

The 11,2 is a form of the 4, so it has the characteristics of the 4, the 11, and the 2. This is a very gentle form of the 4 if it is being lived positively. Also, it is made more intelligent by the 11 and intuitive by the combination of the 11 and the 2. This compound number will probably seek a quiet, gentle way to do a lot of work.

To get a better idea of this personality, look at what numbers are making up the 2. The characteristics of the 2 differ greatly by what numbers were added to form it. For example, a 2, as the sum of a 1 and a 1, might become a leader; but a 2 formed from a 2, 9, 9 probably will not.

The 11,3

Also read the 11, the 3, and the 5.

The 11,3 is a form of the 5, which has the characteristics of the 11 and the 3. This is a very expressive, social, and creative compound, combining the elements of the 3, the 5, and 11. These are all numbers of a personality that likes to be with others and likes social activity, but this compound might cause the personality to follow the group to a great extent. The 11,3 compound has the material influence of the 5 and the spiritual influence of the 11. This can cause conflict within the self.

The 11,4

Also read the 11, the 4, and the 6.

The 11,4 is a form of the 6 and has the characteristics of all three of those numbers. This is a compound that combines an interest in work and family, and possibly higher interests from the 11. Depending on whether it is positive or negative, this compound can be very kind or there can be a harshness. This personality, if negative, could be quite mean due to the negative aspect of the 4, the possible argumentative nature of the 6, and the added tension from the 11.

The 11,4, if positive, will probably be a very good worker. In the case of this compound, the personality may settle for less than it should because of the 4. The 4 can be a limiting number, which works against the potential of the 11. If this happens, the element of the 6 may bring unhappiness, since this number tends to look for the best. The 6 also looks for beauty. The 4 tends to lessen the perfection that the 6 seeks, because as the 6 seeks beauty, the 4 provides a sturdiness and plain appearance.

The 11,5

Also read the 11, the 5, and the 7.

The 11,5 is a form of the 7 and has the characteristics of all three numbers. This 7 is probably going to be more of a joiner than a simple 7 because the 11 tends to like to be with others. It is also probably going to be much more talkative and less serious than a simple 7. A personality with this compound will usually go through periods when the 11 appears to be dominant and others when the 5 appears to be dominant. This is a compound that may experience problems in relationships because the 11 likes to join, the 5 likes to change frequently, and the 7 likes to be alone. This compound will, at times, cause contradiction.

The 11,6

Also read the 11, the 6, and the 8.

The 11,6 is a form of the 8, so it has the characteristics of the 8, the 11, and the 6. This 8 is going to be more spiritually oriented, more sensitive, more people oriented, and more of a giver than a simple 8. The influence of the 11 may conflict with that of the 8 since the 11 is often spiritual and the 8 is material. With the influence of the 6, the 11,6 compound will probably be very stubborn in arguments and will want the best in material things. Family and togetherness will be very important to this form of the 8.

The 11,6 form of the 8 may not be so driven for power and authority as a simple 8. The personality will care more for others.

The 11,7

Also read the 11, the 7, and the 9.

The 11,7 is a form of the 9, so it has the characteristics of the 9 as well as the 11 and the 7. This 9 will probably want to teach in some way because both the 7 and 9 are present in this vibration, and teaching is a possible trait for both numbers. The 11,7 compound may wish to teach about religion or spirituality, as both the 7 and 11 indicate interest in religion. Interest in science, research, or theater may dominate as these are also possible traits of the 7 and 11. Developing these interests would be a way to also fulfill the characteristic of the 9, which seeks a way to give to others. A 7 and 11 compound is somewhat contradictory, as the 7 often likes being alone and the 11 likes to be with others.

The 11,8

Also read the 11, the 8, and the 1.

The 11,8 is a form of the 1, and thus has the characteristics of the 1, the 11, and the 8. This is a 1 that may seem very contradictory at times, as the 11 and 8 are so different. This is a compound that will probably seek leadership in some form, since both the 8 and 1 are present—though the 11 may tone down this drive.

This is a 1 that will probably seek the limelight in some way since the ego of the 1, the spotlight potential of the 11, and the power of the 8 are all present. This is also a 1 that should be very careful in the use of power, as both the 11 and 8 are present. The 11 is thought to be a vibration where the ways of God and right must be taken into account—and is sometimes called a "carrier of the God force." The 11,8, to be lived positively, needs to learn the truth taught in metaphysics that "the greatest form of self-love is to love others."

The 11,9

Also read the 11, the 9, and the 2.

The 11,9 is a form of the 2, so it has the characteristics of the 2, the 11, and the 9. This 2, if positive, will be extremely giving. This is a 2 that may seek to teach, because of the presence of the 9. With the presence of the 9 and 11, it may lead the personality to seek to do humanitarian work. Other directions the personality may seek are religious work, religious teaching, scientific work, or scientific teaching.

This personality may seek the limelight because of the 11. Aviation could be a goal, for a 9 likes to travel and the 11 sometimes is drawn toward aviation. Electronics and the teaching of electronics might be a goal. This 2 will be exceptionally sensitive because all three numbers are very sensitive. The 11,9 is also a 2 that is very intuitive.

The 11,11

Also read the 11 and the 22.
The 11,11 is a form of the 22 or the 4, depending on how it is being lived, so it has within it the characteristics of the 22, the 4, and the 11. The 11,11 is very highly charged with nervous energy and can be greatly disorganized because of this. It can be extremely intelligent, sensitive and kind, if positive. It can be a very gentle 4. The 11,11 tends to not take too much interest in order or cleanliness. The 11,11, because it is a form of the 22, will tend to be dominant and like being with groups, and giving to groups and causes. If positive, the 11,11 will be a hard worker in a quiet way. There may be problems with over-sensitivity, which can produce illness.

If the 11,11 is negative, it could be quite a problem. This might bring in the characteristics of the 4, which can display much anger, even hatred. The negativity of the 4 would be heightened by the double 11, for the 11 is so intuitive. The inclusion of the 11 within a 4 could make a negative personality do more damage than just a simple 4. However, the kindness and gentleness of the 11 and 2 will usually take dominance and override negativity.

The element of the 1 is also present, as the 11 has a double 1 in it. At times, this personality might be quite selfish. Usually, the 11,11 will be gentle, kind, and loving, for it has so much 11 and 2 in it, but be aware of the possible other side.

The 11,11, because it is a form of the 22 or 4, is actually very materially oriented. The 22 likes to collect things and makes the personality like to have many material things, sometimes even hoarding things. Such a personality can be steered to do good with the 11 in a more material way than with a simple 11.

The 11,22

Also read the 11, the 22, and the 33.

The 11,22 is a form of the 33 or 6, so it has the characteristics of these numbers as well as the elements of the 11, 22, and 3. This compound will probably make the personality very giving, if positive. The 11,22 would also want to be with others, as both the 11 and 22 are numbers that like to join with others.

The 33 will probably make the personality very interested in home, family, fashion, children, music, and art. This is a compound that will bring the urge to reach out to others in many ways—the 33 will want to reach out to family, the 22 to humanity and the 11 to God. The 33 also has the element of the 3 within it, so the characteristics of the 3 will show up. There will usually be a love of children and pets and a need to express oneself in some way will be noticeable. Social activity will be very important.

The 11,22 is a very sensitive vibration, so the personality should have much sensitivity if positive. Much intuition or psychic ability may also be present.

The 11,33

Also read the 11, the 33, and the 44.

The 11,33 is a form of the 44 or 8, so it has the characteristics of the 44 or 8, but it also has the elements of the 33, 11, 6, 3, and 2. This compound can make a very good worker and a very strong personality. This is a form of the 8, which is much more social than a regular 8. This vibration can make the personality very giving or very hard—it can go either way.

The 11,33 is the vibration of an extremely good worker, and it can lead the personality into authority. Also, this vibration will usually give much confidence because of the courage and strength of the 6 and 8, which would help in a taking on of authority and in other situations. The 8 will bring a drive to forge ahead.

The 11,33 is a form of the 8, which likes home, family, and just being with others. This vibration makes the 8 much more sensitive than a regular 8.

If negative, this vibration, because of the sensitivity, confidence, and courage it gives out, can cause the personality to be quite negative. The 6 might cause argumentativeness. The 8 might make the person very stubborn; and the 44, because of the 4, could even bring the feeling of hatred.

The 11,44

Also read the 11, the 44, and the 55.

The 11,44 is a form of the 55 or 1, so it has the characteristics of the 55 or 1, but it also has within it the elements of the 44, 11, 8, 4, and 2. The 11,44 will make this 55 much stronger than a regular 55. It could also make the personality more giving than a regular 55 because of the 11.

An 11,44 will probably be a much better worker than a simple 55 because of the element of the 44. The 44 will tone down the characteristics of the 5 and this personality will generally be a more restricted 55 than a simple 55.

An 11,44 could be quite negative. This is because the overall vibration is 1, which can be selfish. There is the added sensitivity of the 11, possible stubbornness of the 8, and possible hatred from the element of the 44. This could be a difficult vibration to live.

Simple Compound Numbers of 22

The 22,1

Also read the 22, the 1, and the 5.

The 22,1 is a form of the 5, so it has the characteristics of the 5, the 22, and 1. This 5 gives the personality many contradictions. The 22 likes being with others, whereas the 1 likes being alone. These two elements will probably make the personality go back and forth between the two urges. Both the 22 and 1 seem to have a natural dominance. That, coupled with the leadership element of the 1 in this compound, will probably bring leadership.

The characteristics of the 5 may bring an instability to that leadership and to other aspects of life. The 5 likes change and may make the personality move from interest to interest. With the 5, this compound would probably involve a lot of physical movement, travel, involvement with humanity in this travel, and lots of adventure.

If negative, the 22,1 could have quite a problem with excesses or with being too dominant. The combining of 22 and 5 might make the personality frequently seek out others for sex, drink, or drugs. The element of the 1 could also add selfishness to the situation and combining the 22 and the 1 may lead to too much dominance. This is a personality that should be aware of both its negative and positive side to be able to regulate self.

The 22,2

Also read the 22, the 2, and the 6.

The 22,2 is a form of the 6, so it has characteristics of the 6, the 22, and 2. This is a 6 that has a built in contradiction. The 22 tends to be dominant, but the 2 is a follower. This personality will probably go back and forth between the two elements. A 6 built from the compound 22 and 2 will also want to be with others almost all of the time—the 22, the 2, and the 6 all like people. This is a situation where the entire personality should be looked at closely to find the other elements comprising it.

The 22,2 has many contradictions built into it. The 6 will give it confidence, while the 2 and negative 22 will give it timidity. The 22 will give dominance, and the 2 will tone down the dominance.

The 22,2 may also be overly concerned with how he or she appears to others. The 6 makes the personality concerned about what things look like, and the 22,2 and 6 will give much desire to be with those very people that the concern centers on.

The 22,3

Also read the 22, the 3, and the 7.
The 22,3 is a form of the 7, so it has the characteristics of the 7, as well as the 22 and 3. The 22 and 3 make this 7 more of a joiner than a simple 7. The 22 and 3 both seek out others, so this is a much more social 7 than usual. The 22 will usually give concern for others and possible dominance. However, a negative 22 can lack confidence, so it might go the other way.

The 22,3 compound is a personality that may like to teach. The 7 likes to teach and the 22 and 3 enjoy people. The teaching of children or the young may be brought out by the 3. Religion, science, or the theater may be areas of interest for this personality. The 7 tends to make an unusual personality, and because of this there may be problems.

The 22,4

Also read the 22, the 4, and the 8.
The 22,4 is a form of the 8, so it has the characteristics of the 8, as well as those of the 22 and 4. The 8 is interested in the material, as are the 22 and the 4. The 22,4 is a very materially oriented compound, but will probably cause the personality to be a hard worker, if positive. All three of the elements of this compound can be good workers and may cause the person to seek a large amount of work.

Both the 8 and 22 give the personality a natural characteristic of dominance. The 4 is often the opposite, so this personality may seek leadership or it may be held back by the 4.

The 22,4 is a very strong combination and can cause much stubbornness because of the 8 and 4. The 22, which is much more giving, may lessen the rigidity of this compound.

If the personality bearing this compound becomes negative, it could be very negative because the 4 can produce hatred and the 8 can make one stubborn. It is the 22 that could keep the 22,4, from getting too negative.

The 22,5

Also read the 22, the 5, and the 9.

The 22,5 is a form of the 9, so it has the characteristics of the 9, the 22, and the 5. The 22 likes to join groups. The 5 enjoys social occasions and parties. The 9 likes humanity. The 22,5 compound will make the personality really like to get out and be with others.

There may be a love of travel with this vibration, as both the 5 and 9 are present. Along with this love of travel the 22,5 will probably like to see all types of cultures and humanity in many different situations. The 22,5 will probably like adventure and change, and it would be very hard to get this personality to stay in one place instead of traveling, moving, or going somewhere.

There might be an urge to teach, as the 9—a teaching vibration—is present, and some fives like to teach, as well. The 22 would enhance this drive with its love of groups and people.

The 22,5 is a very material 9, as both the 22 and 5 are interested in the material. The 5 could make the personality less serious, and make the interest in the material geared toward parties and having a good time.

The 22,6

Also read the 22, the 6, and the 1.
The 22,6 is a form of the 1, so it has the characteristics of the 1, the 22, and 6. The ego of the 1, the dominance of the 22, and the confidence of the 6 are all put together and this compound can produce a very strong, dominant personality.

This is a 1 that will want to lead others and have contradictions to the personality because the 22 and 6 both think of others, but often the 1 thinks of self. This personality will probably appear to be very nice but will often have problems with being overbearing. The 22,6 is a compound that can appeal to large groups of people, though because of the 1, the image that is given off to the group will sometimes change.

This 1 will be very concerned about image and this personality will probably want to be with others more than most ones.

The 22,7

Also read the 22, the 7, and the 11.
The 22,7 is a form of the 11, so it has the characteristics of the 11, the 22, and 7. The 22,7 is a compound that, if positive, will show much concern for the welfare of others. The 22,7 is rather contradictory. The 22 likes to be with others, whereas the 7 wants to be alone. A personality with

this compound will probably go back and forth between these elements.

The 22,7 is more material than a simple 11 because of the influence of the 22, but this compound will probably be very intuitive and very sensitive. With both the 11 and 7 present, this compound may lead the personality to teach or be involved in science, religion, or electronics. With these numbers, there may be a drawing to the theater. Ministerial pursuits may be followed, and writing or research may be of interest. Because of the 22, this compound is capable of doing a lot of work, particularly work that could be for the good of many.

If the potential of the 22 is not lived up to, but is lived as a 4 instead, a lot of good could still be done because of the overall 11. If negative, much harm could be done because of the negative 4. However, the element of the 22 and the overall 11 will usually override the negative aspect of the 4.

The 22,8

Also read the 22, the 8, and the 3.
The 22,8 is a form of the 3 and has the characteristics of the 3, the 22, and the 8. The 22,8 is a very materially oriented and social 3 because of the 22 and 8.

The 22 will make this a more serious 3 than a simple 3, but still very social. This 3 would be more interested in the causes of humanity than a simple 3 because of the 22. A simple 3 usually just likes social activity, while a 22 may seek a cause for that activity.

With both the 8 and 22 present in this compound, the 22,8 will probably make this personality very dominant and can have the ability to rise to authority in groups. Both the 22 and 8 are very strong numbers and the 8 seeks power and authority. A good direction for the 22,8 to go may be to seek power for good causes, as the 22 may bring to the compound a love for humanity or groups.

The 22,8 could be very negative because of the negative aspect of the 4—the lower vibration of the 22—coupled with the strength and possible stubbornness of the 8. The 22,8 can be quite rigid. Usually, the 22 will override the 4, and a 22,8, if feeling negative, will bounce back quickly to being positive.

The 22,9

Also read the 22, the 9, and the 4.

The 22,9 is a form of the 22 and the 4, and also has characteristics of the 9. The 22,9 can be a very giving vibration. Both the 22 and 9 are oriented to giving to humanity, if they are lived in a positive manner.

The 9 brings the desire to teach, as well as to give in other ways. The 22 would enhance that urge with its love of humanity. This personality may have to be careful not to be too giving without considering the needs of self.

The 9 may also give a love of travel and being with all types of people. A 22,9 should get out, travel, see, and be with the humanity of which these two vibrations give the personality a love.

The 22, if lived as a positive 4, will still be able to do a lot of good if coupled with a 9. However, the person's reaching out would probably be on a smaller scale than with a 22.

If negative, the 22,9 could be destructive due to the negative aspect of the 4. The 22 will usually override the 4 and the personality will overcome negativity.

The 22,11

Also read the 22, the 11, and 33.
See the description of the 11,22.

The 22,22

Also read the 44 and 8.
The 22,22 is a form of the 8, so it has the characteristics of the 8, as well as the 22, the 4, and the 2. This is a very material compound because the double 22 is combined with the influence of the 4 and 8. The 22,22 is also a form of the 44.

The 22,22 will make the personality enjoy being with others. With the influence of the 4, there will be a feeling of restriction, especially since the 4 is intensified in a 44.

The 22,22, if positive, will be a very hard worker. There are many work numbers included in this compound: the 22, the 4, the 8, and the 44. This compound will also make the personality very dominant because of the influence of the 8 and 22. These influences may bring a position of power. However, there may be difficulty in the situation because of the influence of the 4, which is not a very social number.

A 22,22 could be very negative. A 44 is a much stronger form of the 4 than a simple 4; and a negative 4 can be very negative, even to the point of hatred. Usually, things will not become that negative, and the influence of the 22 will override the influence of the 4.

The 22,33

Also read the 22, the 33, the 55, and the 1.

The 22,33 is a form of the 1, so it has the characteristics of the 1, the 33, 22, 6, 5, 4, 3, and 2. This is a very strong, freedom-loving form of the 1. This vibration will probably make the personality a better worker than a simple 1, due to the element of the 22.

A 22,33 will probably give confidence because the 33 is a form of the 6. Also, this vibration will be a 1 that is more socially oriented and giving than a simple 1, because of the elements of the 33, 22, 6, 5, 3, and 2.

This 1 could be very domineering because of the 1 and 22, both of which are numbers that will make the personality like to be in charge—a particularly strong trait of the 22. All these vibrations could bring leadership.

Some forms of the 55 are not good workers, but a 22,33 form of the 55 should be a good worker because of the 22. However, this trait may go back and forth between the positive and negative.

The 55 will very much like being with others because of the 22, which likes groups, and the 33, which is very friendly due to the the intensified 3. Parties and other social occasions may be important.

The 22,33 can be very negative and create a difficult personality. The 55 could cause too much spontaneity or too much indulgence in sex, alcohol, or other things that can be misused.

The 33 makes the personality like to argue and the 22, if negative, can bring hatred. This personality might also misuse the leadership that can come with this vibration.

The 22,44

Also read the 22, the 44, the 66, and the 3.

The 22,44 is a form of the 3, so it has the elements of the 3, 6, the 22, and 44. This is a very unusual 3 not at all like a simple 3. This 3 will probably not be as light-hearted as a simple 3 because it has within it many of the characteristics of the 4.

This is a 3 that has the capacity to do a lot of work and rise to a level of authority. This can be a very hard-driving and powerful 3, and at times the personality might appear narrow.

The 22,44 is a very materially oriented 3, as it is made up of a form of the 4 and 8. If positive, this 3 could accomplish a lot, but if negative, this 3 could be a very hardened personality and even prone to hate.

Simple Compound Numbers of 33

The 33,1

Also read the 33, the 1, and the 7.

The 33,1 is a form of the 7 and has the characteristics of the 7, as well as those of the 33, 6, 3, and 1. This vibration will cause the personality to seek isolation, quiet, and perfection. Both the 1 and the overall 7 seek to be alone, while the 1 may also encourage the personality to leadership.

The 33 part of this compound will cause the personality to love family and like children. The 33 will also give confidence and speaking ability.

The negative aspect of this vibration is that it may cause the personality to be too much of a perfectionist, both with self and with others. This could make the 33,1 a difficult vibration to live with.

The 33,2

Also read the 33, the 2, and the 8.

The 33,2 is a form of the 8, so it has the characteristics of the 8, the 33, 6, and 2. This is an 8 that can be very kind and giving. It is more gentle than a simple 8 because of the 2, which makes it one of the more giving forms of the 8.

Because it has both the 6 and the 8, this 8 will show a lot of confidence, which could lead the 33,2 to a place of authority and power. This vibration will also bring a family orientation and the personality will probably like children.

If negative, this 8 may make the personality argumentative and stubborn, though the characteristics of the 2 will tone down arguments. This is an 8 that might back down from an argument more easily than a simple 8. Usually, the combination of the 8 and 6 would make the personality stubborn enough to want to appear to always be right—in this compound the 2 will soften that tendency.

The 33,3

Also read the 33, the 3, and the 9.

The 33,3 is a form of the 9, so it has these characteristics, as well as the elements of the 33, 6, and the 3. The characteristics of the 3 are, of course, very prominent in this vibration, making it very outgoing, talkative, and friendly. It may even be too outgoing.

If positive, this vibration will cause the personality to be a lover of people in many ways—the overall 9 is a vibration of a humanitarian, the 6 likes family, and the 3 likes children.

If negative, the 33,3 could have a problem with the scattering of talents. This is a trait of the 3, which there is so much of in the 33,3. This personality might have problems focusing in on particular goals and finding direction.

The 33,4

Also read the 33, the 4, and the 1.

The 33,4 is a form of the 1, and as such has characteristics of the 1, as well as elements of the 33, 6, 4, and 3. This is a 1 who will be very family oriented and will like children.

The element of the 4 may tone down the authority of this 1. However, this vibration, with the drive of the 1, the confidence of the 33, and the work orientation of the 4, can go far in the world of work and have a good family, also.

If negative, the 33,4 can be too selfish, argumentative, and mean. The most negative aspect of the 4 is hatred, which might make this a very negative combination, if the personality chooses. The 33 could make this personality quite a fighter and the 1 can cause selfishness.

The 33,5

Also read the 33, the 5, and the 11.

The 33,5 is a form of the 11, so it has the characteristics of the 11, the 33, 6, 5, and 3. This will be a very outgoing, light-hearted form of the 11. This 11 will like having a good time and social activity. The 33 will give this 11 much confidence and greater ability to stand up to problems than a simple 11.

The 33,5 could be extremely giving and uplift many. This vibration might even make the personality too outgoing and giving.

If negative, this vibration can cause a lack of thought in the outcome of actions. The 33,5 might do things without contemplation about consequences and be too much of a follower of others instead of following his or her own thought and feeling. This vibration may cause the personality to not see the deeper aspects, problems, and associations of life.

The 33,6

Also read the 33, the 6, and the 3.
The 33,6 is a form of the 3. It has the characteristics of the 3, the 33, and 6. This vibration will probably make the personality enjoy family and children because of the double element of the 6 and the intensified 3. All family, domestic things, and activities will be important to a 33,6.

The 33,6 will make the personality very confident because of the double 6. This can help the personality very much. If negative, this vibration might cause too much of a love of argument. It can at times cause too much confidence, making the personality too overbearing

The 33,7

Also read the 33, the 7, and the 4.
The 33,7 is a form of the 4, so it has the characteristics of the 4, the 33, 7, 6, and 3. This vibration will probably seek perfection, because it has both the 6 and the 7 vibrations.

The overall 4 will probably make the personality a good worker. The 33,7 will strive for excellence in all he or she does. There is a contradiction in this personality. The 7 often seeks to be alone, whereas the 6 is a joiner. This personality will probably go back and forth between these traits.

The 33,7 could become quite negative because of the overall 4 and the love of argument that the 6 will bring. The element of the 7 might, at times, cause the personality to not see things as they really are.

The 33,8

Also read the 33, the 8, and the 5.

The 33,8 is a form of the 5, so it has the characteristics of the 5, as well as those of the 33, 8, and 6. This personality, if positive, will be driven and magnetic toward others of the opposite sex.

This personality will probably want the best of material things because of the 6 and the 8. It is basically a very material vibration, as well as one that will bring a great love of family and family life.

This could be a very negative vibration because of the materiality, the argumentativeness of the 6, and the spontaneity of the 5. Hopefully, the 6 and 5 elements will keep this personality positive for they are generally uplifting vibrations.

The 33,9

Also read the 33, the 9, and the 6.

The 33,9 is a form of the 6, and as such has the characteristics of the 6, the 33, 9, and 3. When positive, this will be an exceptionally outgoing form of the 6, since it is coupled with the 9. This is a very expressive vibration and can be the vibration of good speaking ability, as the 33 will give confidence and the 9 will help the personality reach out.

This vibration will probably cause a great love of family and others in general with the capacity to be very giving and very kind. There may be a lot of confidence found in this personality.

If negative, this vibration can cause a love of argument. There might be a lot of fighting.

The 33,11

Also read the 33, the 11, the 44, and the 8.
See the description of the 11,33.

The 33,22

Also read the 33, the 22, the 55, and the 1.
See the description of the 22,33.

The 33,33

Also read the 33 and the 3.
The 33,33 is a form of the 3, so it has the characteristics of the 3, but also, those of the 33 and 6. This vibration will give the personality confidence because of the element of the double 6. It will also bring a great love of family, children and housepets because of the 3, of which there is an extreme amount in this compound.

If negative, this compound could cause the personality to have too much confidence, be too outgoing, too talkative, and too much of a lover of beauty. Sometimes too much of good things can become negative.

Another negative aspect of the 3 can be a scattering of talents, so the extreme amount of 3 in this compound might bring this on. The personality may have a hard time focusing on which one of many desires and talents to follow.

The 33,44

Also read the 33, the 44, the 7, and the 5.

The 33,44 is a form of the 5, so it has the characteristics of the 5, but also those of the 44, 33, 7, 6, 4, and 3. This compound is a very material vibration and will cause the personality to always want the best.

This personality should be a very good worker because of the element of the 44 and of the 8. There can be much boldness and confidence in the 33,44, which can bring the person into power or authority. The combination of the 33 and 44, which are forms of the 6 and 8, might help bring this power or authority to pass.

The 33,44 can be quite negative. The drive of the 8, the confidence of the 8 and 6, and the possible negativity of the 4, which can bring hatred, might make this a very difficult personality. The 7 can make this person unusual and alone.

Simple Compound Numbers of 44

The 44,1

Also read the 44, the 1, and the 9.

The 44,1 is a form of the 9, and has the characteristics of the 9, 44, 8, 4 and 1. The 44,1 is not a simple 9. The element of the 1 will make this more selfish than a simple 9.

The 9 is a vibration that causes a lot of expansion and outgoing of the personality. In the case of the 44,1, this trait will probably be toned down quite a bit because the 4 tends to act in the opposite way at times—it tends to restrict.

The 44,1 will probably be a good worker and seek leadership. The 9 will make the personality outgoing and the elements of the 8 and 1 can both bring leadership and power.

If negative, this vibration could cause the personality to be very selfish. A negative 9 or 1 can be very selfish.

The 44,2

Also read the 44, the 2, and the 1.

The 44,2 is a form of the 1, so it has the characteristics of the 1, the 44, the 8, 4, and the 2. This is a very strong 1 with the strength and drive of the 44, a form of the 8.

The element of the 2 might tone down the overall 1 of this vibration. The 44 and 8 will probably make the personality a good worker. If the 2 does not tone the 1 down too far, this personality could find power and authority.

There can be much negativity with a 44,2. The 44 and 8 might give a harshness and the overall 1 can cause selfishness. A negative 44,2 can be a very negative, difficult personality.

The 44,3

Also read the 44, the 3, and the 11.

The 44,3 is a form of the 11, so it has the characteristics of the 11, as well as elements of the 44, 8, 4, and 3. This 11 will be much more materially oriented than most elevens because of the elements of the 8 and 4, which are both very material numbers. It is also a much stronger personality than most elevens.

The 44,3 will make the personality very outgoing and friendly as it has both the 3 and the overall 11. A positive 11 vibration causes one to want to join with others, and the 3 vibration seeks friends.

The 44 and the 8, which the 44 produces, will probably cause this personality to be a good worker and one that can rise to authority. If positive, this authority would be kind to others.

The 44,3 could be quite negative. The 11 is a vibration, which brings inspiration, but if negative, it could be the wrong type of inspiration. The 44 in this compound could be very negative and produce a very hard and mean personality.

The 44,4

Also read the 44, the 4, and the 3.

The 44,4 is a form of the 3, so it has the characteristics of the 3, the 44, 8, and 4. This 3 will be quite different from a simple 3 because it has an extreme amount of the 4 in it. This may make it not as light-hearted as threes often are because the 4, and variations of the 4, produce a much more restricted and hard personality than a simple 3.

The 44,4, if positive, will be extremely work oriented as the 4 and 8 produced by the 44 are work oriented numbers.

The 44,4, if negative, could be quite negative due to the element of the 4, which can produce hatred. The 8 can produce stubbornness, so negativity from this vibration could go on and on.

The 44,5

Also read the 44, the 5, and the 4.

The 44,5 is a form of the 4, so the characteristics of the 4, the 44, the 8, and the 5 are all present. This is a form of the 4 that has built-in contradictions; the 4 is the good worker, sometimes restricted and usually down to earth, but the 5 likes change and is a lover of freedom, which sometimes gets in the way of work.

The 44,5 could be a very difficult vibration to live with. It is very materially oriented and could be quite a fighter as there is so much 4 in this vibration coupled with the 8, which can make the personality stubborn, and with the 5, which can make it seek too much change and excitement. This will usually not be a gentle personality unless it is coupled with other, more gentle, vibrations.

The 44,6

Also read the 44, the 6, and the 5.

The 44,6 is a form of the 5, so it has the characteristics of the 5, the 44, the 8, and the 6. This is a 5 that will want the best of material things and be very conscious of what things look like and, if positive, will have a willingness to work to obtain these things. The 8 and 6 will give this personality much courage and drive. The 6 will also soften the other vibrations.

The 44 and overall 8 of the 44 should make this 5 a much better worker than a simple 5—this personality could go far in the right field.

The 44,6 can be very negative. The stubbornness of the 8 and the argumentativeness of the 6 can dominate the compound. The 4 might lead the personality into hatred. Also, because the 6 always wants to be right, a personality could be produced that does not like to back down.

The 44,7

Also read the 44, the 7, and the 6.

The 44,7 is a form of the 6, so it has the characteristics of the 6, the 44, the 8, and the 7. This 44 will probably be a perfectionist because the 8, 7, and 6 are all working together. If positive, this compound should be a very good worker and can rise to a level of authority because of the 8.

Because of the 7, there will be a lot of things happening by chance to this personality. However, the overall 6 will act opposite to the trait of the 7, which causes one to not see things clearly. This personality will go back and forth between the traits of the 7 and the 6.

The 44,7 could be quite negative. Both the 8 and 6 will give the personality much confidence. The 44, the 8 and the 6 could make a very stubborn fighter who will not back down. The perfectionistic tendencies of this personality could pose a problem to self and others.

The 44,8

Also read the 44, the 8, and the 7.

The 44,8 is a form of the 7, so it has the characteristics of the 7, as well as the 44 and 8. This is a 7 that is very different from a simple 7—it is much more material because of the 44 and 8.

This can be a very unusual personality because of the 7. It will be one that likes being alone and dealing with physical things. The 44,8 can do a lot of hard work, and there will probably be a lot of drive and possibly some type of authority.

If negative, this personality could be quite hard and difficult. There is the trait of not seeing things clearly in this compound because of the 7, so there may be a lot of misinterpreting things. The 44, the overall 8, and the second 8 of this compound can make this personality too material, harsh, and stubborn. The 44,8 is not a good personality to argue with.

The 44,9

Also read the 44, the 9, and the 8.

The 44,9 is a form of the 8, so it has the characteristics of the 8, as well as the 44, 9, and 4. This is a more people oriented 44 because it is coupled with a 9, which will cause it to be much more giving than most compounds of 44. This vibration can make the personality a hard worker and outgoing. It could lead to authority.

This vibration might be quite negative because of the negative possibilities of the 44. The 9, however, will tone down the negativity of this vibration since it is a more people oriented, giving vibration.

The 44,11

Also read the 44, the 11, the 55, and the 1.
See the description of the 11,44.

The 44,22

Also read the 44, the 22, the 66, and the 3.
See the description of the 22,44.

The 44,33

Also read the 44, the 33, the 77, and the 5.
See the description of the 33,44.

The 44,44

Also read the 44, the 8, and 7.
The 44,44 is a form of the 7, so it has the characteristics of the 7, as well as the 44, the 8, and the 4. This is an extremely material combination, but it will probably not show up often, as the 44 is rare in a name.

The 44,44 will be a personality that could seem quite hard, strict and immovable at times, and a double 44 can be a very hard combination to live with. When positive, this compound will make the personality a very hard worker with much drive. With a double 8, this person would almost certainly seek authority.

A 44,44 can be extremely negative. The double 8 will cause much stubbornness and the overall 7 might make the 44,44 have difficulty seeing things clearly. The 4 could bring hatred.

Larger Compound Numbers

On rare occasions, there may be larger compound numbers than 44 within a name, such as a compound of 55 or 66. This will come up so seldom that these compounds are not listed here. If one of these compounds should show up in a name that is being analyzed, go back and check all the main number elements that make up the compound.

Chapter Five

Finding Compatibility Between Names

Not only is it important to know the characteristics of each number in a name and each number in different positions in a numerology chart, it is also important to understand the interaction between numbers. How do numbers affect one another? What numbers are compatible with each other?

The numbers in numerology depict energy patterns called vibrations—some work together harmoniously, while others do not. When using numerology to examine the compatibility of names, be sure to work with the entire name and all the parts of the chart, because while one part of the names may be compatible, others may not be.

This chapter describes the relationship between numbers. This relationship, whether it is harmonious or inharmonious, is called the aspect. To look at the compatibility—the relationships or the interactions between numbers—is to look at the aspects of those numbers.

The Aspects of Numbers: How Numbers Relate

The Number 1

1-1   Most often incompatible

Putting together a 1 and a 1 is pairing two vibrations of strong self-interest, and many conflicts could arise. The 1 is a leadership number; to put a 1 and a 1 together makes them compete for leadership as both may wish to be dominant. There could be much struggle of wills here. If two ones find themselves in this situation, they might try putting a lot of space between each other, giving each an area in which they can excel, or working together on a mutual project where they need each other, but neither dominates the other. These steps may make the relationship work.

In the 1-1 combination, look at the types of ones involved—looking at the structure of the entire name and what makes it up. There are many different types of the 1, and where this number is placed within the chart makes a big difference.

1-2   Most often incompatible

In this situation, the 1 will often dominate and lead—to the point at which the 2 tends to get "smothered." The wants and wishes of the 2 and the will of the 2 are usually put in the background of what the 1 desires. The 2 would be better off with a gentler number, which would allow the 2 better self-expression. The 2 is apt to become a doormat in combination with a 1.

When looking at compatibility with this combination, be sure to check the entire name. It makes a difference where the 1 and the 2 are within the chart of the name. Other numbers within the entire name may change the personality structure—other numbers can "tone down" the dominance of the 1 or make the 2 stronger.

1-3   Most often compatible
The 1 and the 3 will most often be compatible. The ability of those with the 3 vibration to express themselves, combined with the number's sociability, can make the 1 less self-centered. The leadership characteristic of the 1 may be helped by the 3. On the other hand, the push for achievement of the 1 will sometimes be hampered by a 3 that is not driven to obtain, but is instead just happy towards life.

1-4   Most often compatible
The 1 and 4 are usually compatible, if they are positive and choose to work together. The orderly, systematic, practical approach of the 4 may help the drive of the 1. On the other hand, the 4 can tend to be a restrictive number that may make a 1 feel held back. If they choose to be negative, this is not a good combination at all—it puts the ego and the self of the 1 together with the potential to hate in the 4. In a work situation, if the relationship is negative, the self of the 1 may try to take advantage of the love of work of the 4—with the 4 doing the one's work.

1-5   Most often compatible, sometimes incompatible

Compatibility between these two numbers has a lot to do with what is trying to be accomplished. For friendship and good times, the 1 and 5 might be quite compatible. If the relationship is not serious, the 5 can be a lot of fun. If it is a situation where the 1 must be the boss, leader, or director, the 1 may not like a 5. The 5 likes freedom so much that they are not easily controlled by the 1 who likes to control. In the case of a serious thinking 5, being led, directed, and sometimes controlled by a 1 may not be a problem. Look at the entire name to help determine if the personality is a serious type.

The one's drive for achievement might also be hindered by the 5 in a different way. The 5 likes change so much that this trait could keep the 1 from reaching his or her goals.

In a marriage situation, the 1 and the 5 might work well. It depends on the positivity or negativity of the partners and their feelings toward dominance. In a traditional partnership, if the 1 is the male and the 5 the female, the combination might work well. However, in this situation the 5 might feel her freedom curtailed through the dominance of the 1. In the 1 and 5 combination, as in any combination, the two parties must look at all the angles, numbers, and possibilities—positive and negative—which make up the name.

1-6   Most often incompatible

The 1 and the 6 may often be in conflict. The 1 will tend to be self-centered, whereas the 6 likes to work with others. The 6 likes to argue, which may conflict with the leadership drive of the 1. In marriage, family life, or any close living situation, if the 6 tends to be a gentle, non-dominant 6, the 1 and 6 may get along well. However, the 6 is usually quite capable of speaking up for himself.

1-7   *Most often incompatible*

There are aspects of the 1 and of the 7 that are in harmony and some that are not. Both the 1 and the 7 like to be alone, and this may not make for a warm relationship. Look closely at what numbers are making up the 1 and the 7. There may also be a problem because the 7 is introspective and often non-worldly, whereas the 1 will usually want to go out and obtain in the world. The 7 may be spiritual, and the 1 is usually materially oriented. The 7 has a curious aspect about it that might cause frustration in trying to obtain things within the material world—with the 7 things have to happen unexpectedly or by chance. For the 1 who likes to go out, strive, and direct, this could become very frustrating.

1-8   *Most often compatible*

These are both achievement oriented numbers. They usually work well together, unless they are vying for power or leadership. They are both strong numbers, so neither would be pushed to the background by the other. The executive, authoritative trait of the 8 can help the 1 obtain what it wants; if the 1 and the 8 work together they could accomplish much. It is when they compete that a 1 and an 8 can have a real problem. Both the 1 and the 8 are very material, which can bring either harmony or disharmony, depending on if the two vibrations are working together. Spiritual and other non-material influences could be left out of a relationship between a 1 and an 8.

If the relationship between the 1 and the 8 becomes negative, it might be quite negative. Both these vibrations produce a strong will and the 8 can be very stubborn.

1-9   Most often incompatible

There is a lot of conflict between a 1 and a 9, because in a way they are opposite. The 1 is the vibration of self-interest. The 9 is the number of a giver. A relationship between a 1 and a 9 may run into trouble if the 9 grows tired of giving. On the other hand, a negative 9 can be very selfish. In the case where the 9 is selfish, the 1 and the 9 will probably not get along at all.

1-11   Most often incompatible

The 1 and the 11 are most often inharmonious because they are very different. The 1 is materialistic, good for dealing with the physical world. The 11 is often spiritual, good for dealing with the non-material. The 1 is usually pursuing self-interests, whereas the 11 is usually a very giving number. Generally, the 1 wants leadership, while the 11 may or may not be a leader.

1-22   Most often incompatible, sometimes compatible

Since the 22 has the element of the 4 within it, the 22 and the 1 can get along, but there will be a problem with dominance. Dealing with and accomplishing things with others is where the 1 and the 22 may have problems because their approach is so different. The 1 wants to seek attainment, while the 22 wants to help the group or humanity, itself. Within a group, the motivation of the 1 may be more of leadership for self rather than helping the group.

1-33   Most often incompatible
The 1 and 33 may often be in conflict. However, it will probably be less conflict than that found with a simple 6 because of the element of the 3, a number that is compatible with the 1.

However, the 1 and 33 will have problems. The 1 thinks of self and the 33 wishes to work with others. They may fight, because the 33 enjoys arguing and the 1 likes to dominate. The arguing might get in the way of the leadership wishes of the 1.

1-44   Most often compatible
The 1 and 44 will usually be compatible, unless they both seek the same position of power or leadership. Both the numbers are achievement oriented and strong.

If the 1 and 44 are working together or in some type of partnership, they could accomplish a great deal. The authoritativeness of the 8 could help the 1 to leadership.

The 2

2-1   Most often incompatible
See 1-2

2-2   Most often compatible, sometimes incompatible
With the 2-2 combination, compatibility depends on the purpose of the relationship. In the 2-2 combination, neither is really the leader. In a friendship, this may make no difference, but in a situation where a leader is clearly needed a 2-2 combination could be difficult, as both are followers. Neither wants to make decisions and have responsibility. There is too much passivity with this combination

and not enough aggressive action if things are meant to be accomplished. Both are very gentle numbers and may get along well in a friendship, but if strength is needed in the relationship there may be a problem. The 2 and 2, however, can be very intuitive with each other.

2-3   *Most often compatible*
The 2-3 is a combination that usually works well together. The 3 can reach out socially and the 2 can follow. The 3 is expressive or creative and the 2 is encouraging. The 3 may make associations and the 2 follows in the background. Basically, the 2 and the 3 work in harmony.

2-4   *Most often compatible*
The 2 and the 4 are generally compatible. The 2 tends to cooperate and follow the 4. The 4 provides structure, order, or a foundation for the gentler 2. If conflicts arise between a 2 and a 4, the 2 will probably back down. In a positive relationship, a 2 might tone down a rough or stern 4. A 4 can sometimes be a contained, non-expressive personality. It can also be insensitive, in which case the 4 would not be compatible with the 2, as the 2 is very sensitive.

2-5   *Most often incompatible*
Compatibility in a 2-5 combination depends a lot on the purpose of the relationship. In a simple friendship, the 2 and 5 may get along well. In a serious relationship, however, there may be problems. The 5 likes freedom—change and more change. The constant change may be hard for a dependent 2 to deal with. The 5 likes to be independent, which would make it difficult for the dependent 2. A 5 may have an unstabilizing effect on a 2.

2-6   Most often compatible

The combination of 2 and 6 works well together and is usually compatible. It is a very good combination for compatibility in marriage, family life, or a close relationship. Both the 2 and the 6 can be very loving, giving vibrations. Both like association with others. A 6 can provide the love and stability a 2 needs. The 6 would also have the confidence and courage that a 2 might lack.

2-7   Most often incompatible

There is a basic conflict built into an association of a 2 and a 7. The 2 wants to be with others, it is the vibration of a joiner; the 7 is a vibration that makes a person prefer to be alone. Another problem is that the 7 tends to be viewed as unusual or different by others. This would make it difficult on a 2, who wants to be accepted by others.

2-8   Most often incompatible, sometimes compatible

The 8 is a much stronger number than the 2, which can make the 2-8 combination difficult. The 8 is a driving force that, if positive, can bring leadership much different from the 2, who usually just wants to cooperate and follow. The power of the 8 can overwhelm the 2. The 8 is also very interested in material gain, whereas the 2 is not that material. The 2 tends to be intuitive.

2-9   Most often compatible

Both the 2 and the 9 are vibrations that cooperate well with others when they are positive. The 9, if positive, is a very giving vibration. The 2 is also giving and is enhanced by the giving of others. A negative 9, on the other hand, is not compatible with a 2 because a negative 9 is a taker rather than a giver.

2-11   *Most often compatible*

The 2 and the 11 are usually compatible. The 11 is a higher vibration of the 2 with added characteristics. The 2 is cooperative, the 11 is an idealist. The 11 can be a leader and this helps the 2, which is a follower. Both the 2 and the 11 are very intuitive. The 11 could lead the 2 into spiritual things or higher thought.

2-22   *Most often compatible, sometimes incompatible*

The 22 carries the element of the 2, so it has some of the characteristics of the 2. This would help in compatibility of the 2 and 22. There are also reasons that the 2 and 22 may be incompatible. The 22 is a very strong, dominant number that may be too dominant for the 2. The 2 and the 22 both like being a part of a group, but the 22 is a strong personality that often leads the group rather than following or blending in. The 22 is a material achiever; the 2 is not. The 22 is a very giving number, so in close associations the 22 and 2 combination might work if the 22 is not too dominant.

2-33   *Most often compatible*

The 2 and 33 will usually be compatible. This is a good combination in family life or close relationships as long as the 33 does not over-dominate. The 2 and 33 are very loving vibrations; both are very giving.

The 33 can provide strength and stability for the 2. It can also provide confidence, which is often lacking in the 2.

2-44   *Most often incompatible*

The 2 and 44 may be incompatible, because the strength of the 44 may overwhelm the 2, which is a gentle follower. The 44 is a form of the 8—it has much drive and force, and will probably push to "get ahead" in life. The 2 will follow along. The 44 is also very material, but the 2 is not.

The 3

3-1   Most often compatible
See 1-3

3-2   Most often compatible
See 2-3

3-3   Most often compatible
A 3 will generally get along well with another 3. They could have a very good time together if both are positive and have a love of life. The interior structure of both the threes should be checked when looking at their potential compatibility, since there are different types of the 3. (This is true with all the numbers.) There may be a problem in communication with two threes, in that the 3 likes to talk. The 3-3 combination may have to learn to listen to the other and talk less. Self-expression is very important to both individuals in this combination.

3-4   Most often incompatible
The 3-4 combination does not work well together. The 4 is so much more contained than the 3 that the 3 may perceive the 4 as holding the 3 back. The 3 likes to self-express and create. The 3 can see the 4 as rigid and unbending. The 4 can see the 3 as frivolous and shallow.

3-5   Most often compatible
Both the 3 and the 5 are very sociable and expressive. Most threes and fives are light-hearted and enjoy life. The 5 will usually like the change and social activity that a 3 can bring

to life if both are living positively. Depending on the whole structure of the names, a 3 and a 5 might have a hard time handling money, as both can spend loosely. They can also have a problem if both are not serious types—it might get hard to accomplish serious things. When checking compatibility in this combination, it is important to keep in mind the type of relationship sought by the personalities.

3-6   *Most often compatible*

Both the 3 and the 6 are very socially oriented and can be very friendly. Both are very creative and expressive numbers. This is usually a good marriage combination, because the 3 likes children and the 6 is very family oriented. What type of 3 and what type of 6 are being analyzed should be closely examined, but the 3 and the 6 are usually very compatible.

3-7   *Most often incompatible, sometimes compatible*

The 3-7 combination puts the expressive vibration 3 with the introspective, reserved vibration 7—contradictory characteristics. Sometimes, a 3 will draw out a 7 and the two vibrations can get along quite well. The 3 and 7 combination is another combination in which the entire structure of the names should be carefully checked. It would take a great deal of understanding for a very social 3 and very reserved 7 to get along for a long period of time.

3-8   *Most often compatible, sometimes incompatible*

Basically, the 3 and 8 have very different orientations. The 8 is very material, achievement oriented, and likes power. The 3, if it is not a 3 built from an 8, just likes to enjoy life in general. The sociability of the 3 might be in opposition to the eight's need of leadership and control. The fixity of the 8 is also very different from the expressiveness of the 3. To determine compatibility or incompatibility between the 3 and the 8, look very closely at all factors involved. The 3 and the 8 will probably simply tolerate each other rather than be incompatible.

3-9   Most often compatible

The 3 and the 9 are usually both very social, expressive vibrations that get along well. Both the 3 and the 9 are people oriented. The 9 likes to give to others and the 3 likes to be with others. Both traits often go together and this combination works very well together. If there is a problem, it may be because they are both very expressive vibrations. They have to learn to let the other talk while they do a little listening.

3-11   Most often compatible

The creativity and expressiveness of the 3 allows it to get along with most other vibrations, including the 11. Generally, the 11 is a much more serious vibration than the 3, which likes social occasions and joy in life. The 11 has an interest in mental or spiritual pursuits, such as religion, science, electronics, or the stage. The 3 and 11, although different, can usually get along because of the ability of the 3 to communicate so well.

3-22   Most often compatible, sometimes incompatible

Whether or not the 3 and the 22 are compatible is often related to how they are being lived, because the 22 can be lived as a 22 or a 4. A 22, lived as a 22, is much more compatible with a 3 than a 22 lived as a 4. The 22 is a much more serious vibration than a 3, and the 22 tends to be a dominant vibration, whereas the 3 does not care about dominance. Both are very social, but in different ways. The 22 is interested in groups and in humanity itself, possibly leading a group or building for the good of humanity. The 3 usually just wants friends. Look at the type of 3 being compared. If the 22 is being lived as a 4, look back at the compatibility description of the 3 and the 4.

3-33   *Most often compatible*
The 3 and 33 are usually compatible. They have many of the same likes, since the 33 has much of the element of the 3. Both the 3 and 33 are very social, friendly, positive vibrations. A marriage between a 3 and 33 is usually very good, provided other points of compatibility are high. The 33 is a form of the 6, which likes family and contains the element of the 3, which cares about children. A simple 3 also likes children.

3-44   *Most often incompatible*
The goals of the 44 and 3 are very different. The 3 is social and wants to enjoy life. The 44 is achievement oriented. The 4 within the 44 is also a reason for incompatibility because the 4 and 3 are usually incompatible. Basically, the 44 and the 3 are just very different.

The 4

4-1   Most often compatible
See 1-4

4-2   Most often compatible
See 2-4

4-3   Most often incompatible
See 3-4

4-4   Most often compatible, sometimes incompatible
The 4-4 combination will be compatible if both are positive. Both will be hard workers, steady and dependable builders. If negativity arises in the 4-4 combination, there could be a lot of fighting. The very negative 4 is prone to hate, so two fours reacting negatively to each other can really hurt each other.

4-5   Most often incompatible
The 4-5 combination is usually not compatible—they basically want two different things. The 4 wants dependability, order, structure, or a system. The 5 wants change after change and lots of freedom. The 5 can easily feel boxed in or stifled by the 4.

4-6   Most often compatible, sometimes incompatible
The 4-6 combination is usually harmonious and both personalities are usually dependable. The 4 tends to seek order, structure, or a system. The 6 is usually a responsible, solid type. They can work together well, but in a romantic relationship the 4 and 6 can run into incompatibility. The 4 often lacks magnetic attraction between the sexes, whereas the 6 values extreme beauty.

4-7   Most often compatible

The 4-7 combination is usually compatible. Neither vibration is very expressive or very dominating, depending on the inner make-up of the vibration. These are two vibrations that will usually just quietly get along. If there is a conflict, it might be because the 7 can be very unusual and the 4 is usually a dependable, "salt of the earth type" that likes to fit in with the norm.

4-8   Most often compatible

The 4 and the 8 are usually compatible vibrations because they are a lot alike. Both are very interested in material things. If positive, both can be very hard workers. The 8 will tend to be dominant, because of its leadership quality and great strength.

4-9   Most often compatible, sometimes incompatible

The 4-9 combination is usually compatible. They tend to get along, but not with extreme compatibility. The 9 may feel held back by the 4. The 4 is a steady worker. The 9 has an interest in teaching, humanity, and travel. The entire structure of the names should be closely checked to determine compatibility between the 4 and 9. Compatibility will probably depend on what the two are trying to accomplish together.

4-11   Most often incompatible

The basic characteristics of the 4 and of the 11 are very different. The 4 is usually interested in the material world. It is a vibration for building systematically in the material world. The 11 is interested in religion, spiritual pursuits, electronics, science, or theater. It is a more mental or spiritual vibration, which may have an impact on the material world. The 11 may see the interests of the 4 as not being on as high a level.

4-22   *Most often compatible, sometimes incompatible*

The 4 and the 22 are usually compatible, as the 22 has the characteristics of the 4. Both vibrations can be very good workers. The interests of the 22 go beyond the interests of the 4. The 4 seeks to steadily and orderly build a foundation in the material world. This will generally be just for family and friends. The 22 extends that interest into wishing to build in the material world, for humanity itself—the 22 seeks to build for the entire group rather than for self.

4-33   *Most often incompatible, sometimes compatible*

Because there is so much 3 within the 33, the 33 will generally be incompatible with the 4, as the 4 and 3 have problems with compatibility. Sometimes the overall 6 of the 33 and the 4 will show compatibility, though—these can both be solid, responsible personalities. Romantic relationships between the 33 and 4 may not work well. The 33 is a form of the 6, which values beauty. The 4 tends to be more solid and sturdy than beautiful.

4-44   *Most often compatible*

The 4 and 44 are usually compatible. The 44 has a lot of the element of the 4. The 44 will, however, be stronger and have much more drive. The 44 is a form of the 8, so it will often have the drive and force of the 8. Both 4 and 44 are numbers of good workers and down-to-earth types. They are very material vibrations.

The 5

5-1   Most often compatible, sometimes incompatible
See 1-5

5-2   Most often incompatible
See 2-5

5-3   Most often compatible
See 3-5

5-4   Most often incompatible
See 4-5

5-5   Most often incompatible, sometimes compatible
The compatibility of the 5-5 combination depends on the purpose of the relationship. The 5-5 combination may want too much freedom. This relationship, if negative, may over-indulge in drink, sex, or drugs. Short-term relationships or simple friendships might work well, but a long-term, serious relationship will probably have trouble. The 5 likes change, so two fives together will often seek so much change that it would jeopardize or erode any foundations they set up.

5-6   Most often incompatible
The 5 and 6 vibrations are very different, which often makes them incompatible. The 6 is a vibration that can take on responsibility and show concern for others. The 5 likes change and freedom, and often disregards responsibilities. In a marriage situation a 5 and 6 might get along because the 6 likes family and the 5 likes sex. However, the 6 would probably have to be very tolerant with a 5 companion.

5-7   *Most often incompatible*

The 5 is not at all as serious as the 7. The 7 tends to like quiet, research activities, and being alone. The 5 seeks social situations and is usually just too social for a 7. In short-term relationships, the 5 and the 7 may get along.

5-8   *Most often incompatible, sometimes compatible*

The basic interests of the 5 and the 8 are very different in some ways, and in others very alike. Both are very materially oriented vibrations, however, their approach to material things is very different. The 5 likes to have good times with the material, while the 8 seeks power and authority with it. Also, the 8 likes to accumulate wealth—the 8 is a builder in the material and a very fixed vibration. The 5 likes freedom, which is in conflict with the fixity of the 8.

5-9   *Most often compatible, sometimes incompatible*

Both the 5 and 9 like to travel and have a lot of freedom. They like to get out and go and can make good companions. Conflict may come into the relationship because of the five's desire for freedom conflicting with the people helping trait of the 9.

5-11   *Most often incompatible*

The 5 and the 11 are very different. The 5 is usually light-hearted, while the 11 is serious. The 5 likes material things for having a good time, and the 11 is more spiritually or mentally oriented. The 11 is a vibration that makes the personality live more for others if it is lived positively. The 5 tends to like to have a good time for self.

5-22   Most often compatible, sometimes incompatible
The 5-22 compatibility depends on how the 22 is being lived—whether as a 22 or as a 4. A 22 lived as a 22 is more compatible with a 5 than a 22 lived as a 4. A 22 lived as a 22 likes people, as does a 5, but probably for different reasons. The 22 is much more serious and likes helping people. A 22 may seek to lead a group. The 5 just likes to have a good time with people, whether it is one-on-one or in groups. If the 22 is being lived as a 4, check the 4-5 combination for that indication of compatibility—one in which the 5 and 22 would have little compatibility.

5-33   Most often incompatible, sometimes compatible
The 5 and 33 can be quite different, thus they are often incompatible. The 33 is a form of the 6, and the 6 and 5 can be very different. The 5 likes freedom and lots of change and sometimes disregards responsibility. The 6 is a vibration that can handle a lot of responsibility. A marriage between a 33 and 5 might work, however. The 5 likes sex and the 33 likes family. The element of the 3 in the 33 will also make the 33 more compatible to a 5 than a simple 6.

5-44   Most often incompatible, sometimes compatible
The 5 and 44 might at times be compatible because both are very material numbers. The 44, however, has a lot of 4 in it, which makes it incompatible to the 5. This can make the 5 and 44 often in conflict. The 44 is a very rigid, fixed vibration, whereas the 5 is usually a freedom lover and likes change.

The 6

6-1   Most often incompatible
See 1-6

6-2   Most often compatible
See 2-6

6-3   Most often compatible
See 3-6

6-4   Most often compatible, sometimes incompatible
See 4-6

6-5   Most often incompatible
See 5-6

6-6   Most often compatible
The 6-6 relationship will be two personalities interested in home and family. If other factors surrounding them are compatible, they could have a very good relationship and very good home life. If they are negative, they would probably argue a lot and each would be stubborn, believing that they are right.

6-7   Most often incompatible
The 6-7 relationship will usually not be compatible because the 6 likes to be with others and the 7 prefers to be alone. The 6 can make the personality very giving, while the 7 tends to make the personality aloof, living within self. The 6 needs more demonstrations of affection than the 7 can give.

6-8   Most often compatible

The 6-8 relationship is often compatible. The 6 and 8 can get along, depending on the relationship. If positive, both like quality in the material world. The 8 can acquire power and authority, while the 6 can be a good supportive vibration for this 8.

6-9   Most often compatible

The 6-9 relationship is usually compatible. The 6 and 9 are able to handle a lot of responsibility towards others. Both these vibrations make the personality loving. There may be a conflict in the focus on giving in the 6 and 9. The 6 likes to give to family and friends. The 9 likes to give, as a humanitarian, on a larger scale than just to family and friends.

6-11   Most often compatible

The 6-11 relationship is usually compatible. Both the 6 and 11, if positive, have a lot of concern for others, but it is expressed in different ways. The 6 shows concern for family and friends. The 11 often shows concern for others through an interest in religion, science, or the stage. The 11 is a born giver, which is what the 6 needs, as the 6 can be very affectionate.

6-22   Most often compatible

The 6-22 relationship is usually compatible. Both the 6 and the 22, if positive, have much concern for others. The 22 wants to give to humanity in a concrete, material way. The 6 wants to give to family, friends, and home. As long as home and family responsibilities do not get in the way of the twenty-two's larger scale giving, the 22 and the 6 would get along. A problem might arise in a 22 feeling tied down or because the 22 is often very dominant.

6-33   *Most often compatible*
The 33 is a form of the 6, so it will usually be compatible with a simple 6. The 33 is really an intensified form of the 6 with the element of the 3 added, so these two vibrations are very much alike. Both the 33 and 6 are very interested in home and family. If the other vibrations making up the name are compatible, the 33 and 6 could have a very good relationship and happy home. If the 33 and 6 are negative, they could fight and argue a lot.

6-44   *Most often compatible*
The 6 and the 44 will often be compatible if they are positive. All the elements of the 44 are rather agreeable with those of the 6. A problem may arise, however, because the 44 is not a vibration that usually makes a person attractive and the 6 is a lover of beauty. There probably will not be extreme compatibility between the 44 and 6, but unless they happen to fight, it will be enough to get along. If the 44 and 6 should fight, it could be extreme because the 6 has much confidence and likes things to be perfect. The 44 may also have a lot of confidence, because of the overall 8, and can be very stubborn. The element of the 4 in the 44 could bring hatred. For these reasons, the 44 and 6, if fighting, could be very negative.

The 7

7-1   Most often incompatible
See 1-7

7-2   Most often incompatible
See 2-7

7-3   Most often incompatible, sometimes compatible
See 3-7

7-4   Most often compatible
See 4-7

7-5   Most often incompatible
See 5-7

7-6   Most often incompatible
See 6-7

7-7   Most often incompatible
A 7-7 relationship is usually not compatible. The 7 makes a personality very self-contained, introspective, and aloof. Two sevens together will not reach out much to each other. It would be hard for this combination to overcome their innate reserve in order to build a good relationship. If the two of them were together for a long period of time, a relationship might grow, but there would probably still be a lot of reserve.

7-8   Most often incompatible
The 7 and 8 are very different. The 7 is an introspective vibration, which gives interests more mental or spiritual than the 8. The 8 is interested in achievement in the material world, in power and authority. A 7 and an 8 will seldom seek a relationship with each other.

7-9   Most often compatible, sometimes incompatible
Depending on the situation, a 7 and 9 might be compatible. Both the 7 and 9 have potential to teach in spiritual pursuits, science, or some area of study and research. These potentials can draw them together. The giving and expressiveness of the 9 can draw out a 7 to form a relationship. In most other situations, a 7 and 9 may have a hard time forming a relationship.

7-11   Most often compatible
The 7 and the 11 are both vibrations that give an interest in religion, God, and spiritual pursuits. This can draw the 7 and 11 together. Neither the 7 nor the 11 are very materially oriented, which might produce a problem in dealing with the world.

7-22   Most often incompatible, sometimes compatible
The 7 and the 22 give personalities very different traits. The 22 likes to be with others, whereas the 7 likes to be alone. The 22 reaches out to a group or to humanity. The 7 is introspective. The 7 and 22 probably will not form a relationship very often.

7-33   Most often incompatible
The 7 and the 33 are usually not very compatible. The 33 enjoys being with others, but the 7 likes to be alone. The 33 will tend to make the personality outgoing and giving. The 7 tends to be aloof and self-contained. In a relationship, a 33 will probably feel a need for more affection than a 7 can give. Also, the 33 will seek family relationships, but the 7 may wish to live alone.

7-44   Most often incompatible
The basic interests of the 7 and 44 are different. The 7 is
an introspective vibration, whereas the 44 is a very material and work oriented vibration. The 7 may be interested in
study, religion, theater, or science—all of which are much
more mental pursuits than those enjoyed by the 44.
Because of the differences in interests, a 7 and a 44 will seldom seek relationships.

The 8

8-1   Most often compatible
See 1-8

8-2   Most often incompatible, sometimes compatible
See 2-8

8-3   Most often compatible, sometimes incompatible
See 3-8

8-4   Most often compatible
See 4-8

8-5   Most often incompatible, sometimes compatible
See 5-8

8-6   Most often compatible
See 6-8

8-7   Most often incompatible
See 7-8

8-8   Most often compatible, sometimes incompatible
The 8-8 relationship is usually compatible, depending
upon the situation. The 8 is a very materialistic number.

Where there is no competition between the two, they should get along well. Placing two eights in competition for leadership and power, two things the 8 seeks, will probably create incompatibility. Two eights together may also put too much emphasis on the material, leaving mental and spiritual pursuits out.

8-9   *Most often incompatible*
The 8 and 9 are very different. The 8 deals with material pursuits, while the 9, if positive, is a humanitarian giver. The 8 seeks power and material wealth. The 9 seeks to give to people and social causes.

8-11   *Most often incompatible*
The 8 and 11 are vibrations that can attract one another, but they are very different. The 8 deals with the material. The 11 deals with the spiritual or mental.

8-22   *Most often compatible, sometimes incompatible*
The 8 and the 22 are both interested in the material world, though the direction of interest may be different. The 8 seeks power and wealth. The 22 seeks to build within the material for humanity or for a group. Both can make very strong, powerful personalities.

8-33   *Most often compatible*
The 8 and 33 will usually be compatible, but whether or not they get along depends on the type of relationship. Both the 8 and 33 like to seek quality and can be strong, confident vibrations, if positive. They could be very supportive of each other, or go the other way and be in much conflict.

8-44   Most often compatible
The 8 and 44 are much alike, since the 44 is a form of the 8. The 44 may have more drive than a simple 8, but the element of the 4 can keep this form of the 8 in a lower position of authority than a simple 8. Both the 44 and the 8 are very material, achievement, and work oriented vibrations.

The 9

9-1   Most often incompatible
See 1-9

9-2   Most often compatible
See 2-9

9-3   Most often compatible
See 3-9

9-4   Most often compatible, sometimes incompatible
See 4-9

9-5   Most often compatible, sometimes incompatible
See 5-9

9-6   Most often compatible
See 6-9

9-7   Most often compatible, sometimes incompatible
See 7-9

9-8   Most often incompatible
See 8-9

9-9   Most often compatible
The 9 in relationship to another 9 is usually compatible, if both are positive. The 9 is very expressive and likes to give.

Both will be givers in a relationship, and communication will usually flow freely. Check the entire structure of the names to see what type of 9 is being examined.

9-11   *Most often compatible*
Both the 9 and the 11 make the personalities very giving. Both are interested in things beyond the self, if positive. The 9 tends to make the personality humanitarian, often getting involved in social causes. The 11 can be religious or scientific, and seeks to help people through these avenues.

9-22   *Most often compatible*
The 9 and the 22 are both humanitarian personalities, if lived positively. They make the personality wish to give to humanity. The 22 extends that wish to building in the material for humanity, while the 9 may seek to teach.

9-33   *Most often compatible*
The 9 and 33 are usually compatible. Both are generally very outgoing and concerned about others. These vibrations can make personalities very loving and giving, though the focus of the giving of a 9 and a 33 may be different. The 9 will tend to give to humanity as a whole. The 33 will tend to give to family and children.

9-44   *Most often incompatible*
The 9 and 44 are often incompatible because they are different. The 44 tends to be very materially oriented, the 9 is oriented to help humanity. If positive, it is a vibration that causes the personality to be very giving. The 44 will probably be a very good worker and a seeker of authority and power. The 9 will seek to serve and give.

The 11

11-1   Most often incompatible
See 1-11

11-2   Most often compatible
See 2-11

11-3   Most often compatible
See 3-11

11-4   Most often incompatible
See 4-11

11-5   Most often incompatible
See 5-11

11-6   Most often compatible
See 6-11

11-7   Most often compatible
See 7-11

11-8   Most often incompatible
See 8-11

11-9   Most often compatible
See 9-11

11-11 Most often compatible
A relationship between two 11 personalities is usually compatible. However, they might give to one another too much. Another problem is that sometimes the 11 is a leader, and sometimes a follower. Two elevens together would have to have one willingly be the follower and one be the leader.

11-22   Most often compatible, sometimes incompatible
The 11 and the 22 are usually compatible vibrations. Both seek to help others and are very good, kind, and giving vibrations. If there is a conflict in these two vibrations, it may arise because the 22 is more materially oriented than the 11.

11-33   Most often compatible
The 11 and 33 are most often compatible. Both the 11 and 33, are very oriented to helping others and can be very giving. The 33 will be more specifically oriented to giving to family and children, while the 11 will be giving in general and interested in religion, theater, electricity, aviation, social work, teaching, or similar professions.

11-44   Most often incompatible
The 11 and 44 are most often incompatible because their orientations are so different. The 44 is very material, whereas the 11 is usually spiritually oriented. These are two vibrations that may attract one another, but in the end they are very different.

The 22

22-1   Most often incompatible, sometimes compatible
See 1-22

22-2   Most often compatible, sometimes incompatible
See 2-22

22-3   Most often compatible, sometimes incompatible
See 3-22

22-4   Most often compatible, sometimes incompatible
See 4-22

22-5   Most often compatible, sometimes incompatible
See 5-22

22-6   Most often compatible
See 6-22

22-7   Most often incompatible, sometimes compatible
See 7-22

22-8   Most often compatible, sometimes incompatible
See 8-22

22-9   Most often compatible
See 9-22

22-11   Most often compatible, sometimes incompatible
See 11-22

22-22   Most often compatible, sometimes incompatible
The 22 and the 22 will usually get along because they are very giving vibrations if they are both being lived as a 22 rather than a 4. If a conflict arises, it may be because the 22 tends to be a dominant vibration. Two twenty-twos together may have a problem with who will be dominant in the relationship.

22-33   Most often compatible, sometimes incompatible
The 22 and 33 are usually compatible in most areas, though they may have difficulty living together because the 22 may be messy, and the 33 likes things neat. Both are concerned for others, however, the focus of concern differs. The 22 is concerned for groups and humanity. The 33 is usually more concerned for family and children.

22-44   Most often compatible
The 22 and 44 are a lot alike, so they are usually compatible. Both the 22 and 44 have the element of the 4 in them, giving them characteristics of this number and making them both very materially oriented. The 22 will help others more than the 44, because of the 2 element. The 44 will be more oriented to seeking authority and power. Both vibrations may tend to dominate others.

The 33

33-1   Most often incompatible
See 1-33

33-2   Most often compatible
See 2-33

33-3   Most often compatible
See 3-33

33-4   Most often incompatible, sometimes compatible
See 4-33

33-5   Most often incompatible, sometimes compatible
See 5-33

33-6   Most often compatible
See 6-33

33-7   Most often incompatible
See 7-33

33-8   Most often compatible
See 8-33

33-9   Most often compatible
See 9-33

33-11   Most often compatible
See 11-33

33-22   Most often compatible, sometimes incompatible
See 22-33

33-33   Most often compatible
The 33 and 33 are, of course, most often compatible if they are simple numbers because they are usually alike. The entire structure of the vibration should be checked to see if other vibrations are making up the 33, or if it is a simple 33. The structure of a 33 might change its compatibility to other forms of the 33.

33-44   Most often incompatible
The 33 and 44 are at first compatible, but they may run into conflict since the 33 has the element of the 3 and the 44 has the element of the 4—a combination that is not very compatible. However, the overall 6 of the 33 and the overall 8 of the 44 are compatible. There will probably be a going back and forth between compatibility and non-compatibility for these two vibrations.

The 44

44-1   Most often compatible
See 1-44

44-2   Most often incompatible
See 2-44

44-3   Most often incompatible
See 3-44

44-4   Most often compatible
See 4-44

44-5   Most often incompatible, sometimes compatible
See 5-44

44-6   Most often compatible
See 6-44

44-7   Most often incompatible
See 7-44

44-8   Most often compatible
See 8-44

44-9   Most often incompatible
See 9-44

44-11   Most often incompatible
See 11-44

44-22   Most often compatible
See 22-44

44-33   Most often incompatible
See 33-44

44-44   Most often compatible
The 44-44 combination is usually compatible if it is a simple 44 because they are alike. With this combination, examine the entire structure of the 44 to determine compatibility. The structure of some forms of the 44 may alter the compatibility.

Note: When checking compatibility, be sure to remember to check each name and each part of the name. Use numerology and the above lists as guidelines. There are many factors to consider when assessing compatibility. It is not a simple process and those books that over-simplify this process can do more harm than good.

Putting the Parts Together

So far, we have learned to break down a name, compare that name to another, and to assess the compatibility between the two names (for reference, turn back to the charts on pages 37 and 51). Look at all the parts, then refer back to the definitions of what the numbers mean and how the numbers relate to one another to refresh your memory. This is how to use numerology to determine basic innate compatibility. However, it is only a beginning; there are other important things to know in order to completely determine compatibility. First, let's go over the importance of a part of the numerology assessment—the soul urge.

The Heart Vibration or Soul Urge

One very important part to consider in determining compatibility is the heart vibration, or soul urge, of the people whose vibrations you are assessing for compatibility. This is of such great important that it will again be mentioned in this section.

This is important because, as you will learn from numerology, there is a part of a person that he or she will appear to the world to be, and then there is the part that the person is within his or her heart. The part the person will appear to be is the inner self. The part that is within the heart is the soul urge. You will find a person seems to go back and forth between these parts.

However, you will find that in the difficult times of life, what a person is in his or her heart will override the other parts. This will happen over and over, so when checking for compatibility, give the soul urge (heart vibration) some of the greatest importance. Two people with conflicting soul urges may in time show incompatibility even when the other parts of their vibrations are very compatible.

One Problem—Reverse or Negative Vibrations

One problem that is important to know about and to look for is the fact that vibrations can act in reverse or negatively. "Reverse" means that as strong as a good vibrational match can be for a positive relationship, it can also be just as strong for a negative relationship. It is interesting to find that some of the people you do not get along with are potentially those that you could have a very good, positive relationship with. The keyword is positive. If you reverse your feeling about someone you feel very negatively toward, you may find there are vibrations for a good relationship. When analyzing compatibility, look at all possible angles.

Also very important is the fact that true compatibility is vibrational. A knowledge of vibrational compatibility will show you that the culturally defined appearances of compatibility often are not true. Examples of true compatibility will be found, regardless of age, race, sex, or other culturally defined barriers.

Often, the culture you live in and the ideas you have been taught actually hold you back from true love and compatibility. As you learn about compatibility by vibration, you should also grow in your tolerance of others. It becomes evident that the being, or force, called God set up a system of compatibility much wider and greater than man-made cultural systems.

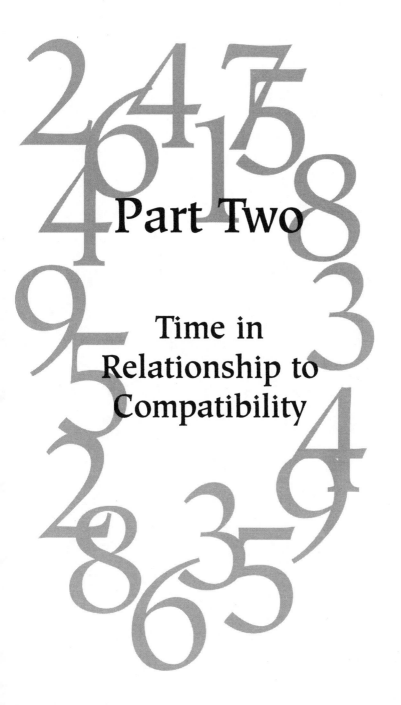

Part Two

Time in Relationship to Compatibility

Chapter Six

Introduction to the Vibrations of Time and How to Chart Them

An important factor to consider in determining vibrations is the element of time. Every day, every week, every month, and every year has a vibration that can be shown by numerology. This vibration changes as the time changes.

The vibrations of a time period are what can be used to bring different things into your life. A knowledge of the vibrations of time can help you obtain material objects, enhance existing relationships, or help form new ones. With a knowledge of the vibrations of time you can know when to look for the things you want in the material world. This includes the wish for compatibility, friendship, or love. For the purposes of this book, the focus will be on the vibrations that can bring compatibility, friendship, or love.

Vibrations of Time in Relationship to Compatibility

As stated before, every day, week, month, and year has a vibration. Some of these vibrations are better for looking for or developing compatibility than others. Often, people fall in love or form friendships because of the vibrations they are under, rather than the vibrations that they are. A full knowledge of vibrations of compatibility should combine a knowledge of the personal innate vibrations (as described in Part I) with a knowledge of the vibrations of time. If the people being analyzed have innate vibrations that are compatible, it is still very important to know the vibrations of the time period. At certain times compatibility is enhanced, but at other times the negative aspect of certain vibrations can override even the best of innate compatibility.

A Problem: One Possible Cause of Divorce

A very important reason to understand vibrations of time periods in relationship to compatibility is that often two people whose innate vibrations are not really compatible will come together at a time when vibrations can produce love. Later, when the vibrations change and are no longer loving vibrations, they will lose that love. This is one cause of divorce. With a knowledge of vibrations, intelligent, creative people can learn to avoid this. With numerology you can learn how to make relationships that will be both satisfying and lasting.

Every relationship is different, and some can withstand conflicts more than others. Knowledge of vibrations, along with compassion and creativity, can make many relationships better. This can give new life to a failing relationship, or help you to know if the relationship is worth trying to salvage. A knowledge of vibrations can bring deeper understanding between people.

Value of the Use of Time Vibrations to Look for Compatibility

There are many reasons that learning how to use the vibrations of time can help in a search for compatibility or love. This knowledge can help save time and eliminate a lot of pain in building relationships. It can help you understand the relationships that you are in, tell you what type of relationship you have, and its probable outcome. The maintenance of a relationship can be helped by a knowledge of vibrations.

Another value in learning how to use both innate compatibility and the vibrations of time, as taught by numerology, is that this knowledge can give a deeper appreciation of what we call God. Numerology is a number system that depicts vibrations. When you use it to examine and verify compatibility, it shows how there must have been an intelligence beyond our comprehension to set up this system to begin with. This intelligence, whether it is a being or a force, must be God.

Many good things could come from this knowledge if it is used correctly. A true and lasting love will have an innate similarity in vibration or vibrations. Relationships that do not last, or are very difficult to live with, will have some point of innate vibrational incompatibility. Relationships formed under time vibrational compatibility will be found to last as long as the time vibrations last, but problems will arise when the time vibrations change.

To find the vibrations of time in examining compatibility, it is necessary to create a time chart. How to create a time chart will be shown step-by-step in this chapter. Before this, however, is a review of addition, an explanation of how to subtract in numerology, and some basic definitions of terms used in a chart. The addition, subtraction and definitions will aid in learning how to make a time chart.

A Review of Addition in Numerology

Before beginning, you may want to go back and look over the previous discussion of addition in Part I, beginning on page 14. A summary is also provided here.

Adding Main Nine Numbers and Main Nine Numbers

Main nine numbers are added to other main nine numbers like simple arithmetic (i.e., 1+3 = 4).

Adding Main Nine Numbers and Master Numbers

Main nine numbers are added to master numbers by adding the master numbers alone and the main nine numbers alone. The sums are then separated with a comma (i.e., 2+11+3+22=33,5).

Adding Main Nine Numbers and Compound Numbers

Main nine numbers are added to compound numbers by adding the main nine number and the main nine number part of the compound number (i.e., 1+22,3 = 22,4).

Adding Master Numbers and Master Numbers

Master numbers are added to master numbers like simple arithmetic (i.e., 11+22 = 33).

Adding Master Numbers and Compound Numbers

Master numbers are added to compound numbers, by adding the master number to the master number part of the compound number. The main nine number part of the compound is left alone (i.e., 11+11,7 = 22,7).

Adding Compound Numbers and Compound Numbers

Compound numbers are added to other compound numbers by adding the main nine number part of the two compounds together, and the master number part of the two compound numbers together (i.e., 11,4+22,3 = 33,7).

How to Subtract in Numerology

Subtracting is not a function usually taught in numerology, perhaps because it is seldom used. However, there is one place where subtraction is used in a numerology chart of time—to find the attainment for each month.

Because it is not often used, it is difficult to find information on how to subtract in the existing literature about numerology. This is especially true when the subtraction involves master or compound numbers.

In the charts shown in this book, read the master numbers as their lower vibrations because it is easiest to understand, because the master numbers are often lived at their lower vibration, and because it lessens confusion when subtraction is needed in the charts.

Always subtract the lower number from the higher number, regardless of which number appears first. This often means that the master numbers in subtraction are lower than the main nine numbers, since the master numbers are being read as their lower vibration.

In this book, we will reduce master numbers to their simpler form, but they can actually be read in two ways—as master numbers or as simple numbers. This means that it is possible to have more than one answer in subtraction in numerology. This is why it is important to determine if the person who you are doing a chart for is living life as a master number or as a simple number.

Remember: There is often more than one way to subtract in numerology. This is because sometimes master numbers can be lived at their lower vibration.

Subtraction Examples

Subtracting Main Nine Numbers and Main Nine Numbers

Subtract the numbers as in simple arithmetic—but always subtract the smaller number from the larger. There are no negative numbers in numerology.

Example

$$9-8 = 1$$

Example

$$2-7 = 5$$

Subtracting Main Nine Numbers and Master Numbers

First reduce the master number to its lower vibration, then subtract the lower number from the higher number.

Example

$$11-9 = 2-9$$
$$9-2 = 7$$

Example

$$22-3 = 4-3$$
$$4-3 = 1$$

Subtracting Main Nine Numbers and Compound Numbers

First reduce both master numbers and compound numbers to their main nine number equivalent. Then subtract the lower number from the higher number. This is one time when reducing a master number to its lower vibration is needed.

Example

$$11,7-3 = (2+7)-3$$
$$9-3 = 6$$

Example

$$7-22,6 = 7-(22+6) = 7-(4+6) = 7-1 = 6$$

Subtracting Master Numbers and Master Numbers

Master numbers can be subtracted from master numbers as they are, or can be first reduced to their main number form. The lower number is always subtracted from the higher number.

Example

$$11-22 = 2-4$$
$$2-4 = 2$$
or $$11-22 = 11$$

Example

$$33-22 = 6-4$$
$$6-4 = 2$$
or $$33-22 = 11$$

Subtracting Master Numbers and Compound Numbers

To subtract master numbers and compound numbers, first reduce both master numbers and compound numbers to their lower vibrational form (their main number equivalent). Then subtract the lower number from the higher number. This is one time when master numbers must be reduced in numerology.

Example

$$11,5-11 = (11+5)-2$$
$$(2+5)-2 = 7-2$$
$$7-2 = 5$$

Example

$$11\text{-}22,8 = 2\text{-}(22+8)$$
$$2\text{-}(4+8) = 2\text{-}3$$
$$2\text{-}3 = 1$$

Subtracting Compound Numbers and Compound Numbers

The way to subtract compound numbers is to first reduce the compound number to its simple main number equivalent. In subtraction, master numbers are often reduced to their lower vibrational form for easier understanding.

Example

$$11,3\text{-}22,5 = (11+3 = 2+3 = 5)\text{-}(22+5 = 4+5 = 9)$$
$$5\text{-}9 = 4$$

Example

$$11,7\text{-}22,1 = (11+7 = 2+7 = 9)\text{-}(22+1 = 4+1 = 5)$$
$$9\text{-}5 = 4$$

Definitions Used in a Time Chart

Attainment

What can be obtained, or attained, during the month is called the attainment. In the numerology chart for assessing times to seek compatibility, the attainment is found in the bottom triangle.

Compound Numbers

When a main nine number and a master number are combined, or sometimes when a master number and a master number are combined, what is formed is called a compound number. Compound numbers are written with a comma between the parts of the number. Compound numbers are formed because master numbers are not reduced. Examples of compound numbers are (11,3), (11,8), (22,1), (33,4), or (44,2).

Day Digit

The day digit is the numerology equivalent of the number of a day. It has to be reduced as far as possible. The day digit may be one of the main nine numbers or a master number.

Descriptor Numbers

Descriptor numbers are numbers that are not for finding compatibility by themselves, but can help describe a good number for compatibility. Descriptor numbers are 1, 4, 7, 8, and 44. Descriptor numbers can be simple numbers or part of a compound number.

Month Digit

The numerology number for the month is called the month digit. It is reduced as far as possible. The following table shows the month digits.

The month of November is the only one that is different, as it has two possibilities. The 11 of the number for November can be either an 11 or a 2. Try to tell if the person you are doing a chart for is living as a 2 or as an 11 before deciding whether to use the master number or its lower vibration—or draw up charts showing both.

January	1	February	2
March	3	April	4
May	5	June	6
July	7	August	8
September	9	October	10 = (1+0) = 1
November	11 = 1+1 = 2 or 11		
December	12 = 1+2 = 3		

Personal Year

The numerology number for how a year will affect you or another personally is called the personal year. The personal year is obtained by finding the universal year and then adding it to the month and day of birth, which should first be reduced as far as possible. For example, to find the personal year in 2035 for a person born August 14, 1979, follow the steps listed below.

1. Find the universal year for 2035.

   $$2+0+3+5 = 10$$
   $$10 = 1 + 0 = 1$$

2. Add the universal year to the month and birthday digit. The month and birthday digit should be already reduced.

   1 (universal year)
   +8 (month digit for August)
   +5 (birthday digit)
   ___
   14
   $$14 = 1+4 = 5$$

The personal year for a person born August 14, 1979, in the year 2035 is 5.

Simple Numbers

Simple numbers are the main nine numbers as they stand alone, or the master numbers as they stand alone.

Universal Year

The universal year is the numerology number for a particular year and is the same for everyone. The universal year is found by adding the digits of a year and then reducing them as far as they can be reduced in numerology terms.

Example

$$2009 = 2+0+0+9 = 11$$
$$2035 = 2+0+3+5 = 10 = 1+0 = 1$$

Week Digit

The week digit is the numerology number for the vibration of a specific week. It may be one of the main nine numbers, a master number, or a compound number.

Week digits vary. To find the week digit of the first 7 days of the month, add the month digit and the personal year in the numerology chart for looking for compatibility. In a chart, this is position A and B added together.

To find the second week (the 8th to the 14th), add the personal year and third number in the base line of the numerology chart. This is position B and C.

To find the third week (the 15th to the 21st, including the 21st), add the week digits for week 1 and week 2. This is position D and E added together to equal position F.

To find the last part of the month, which is often longer than a week (the 22nd to the end of the month), add the month digit and the third number in the base line. This is position A and position C.

A Sample Time Chart for Using Numerology to Look for Compatibility

This section shows what a blank numerology chart for looking for compatibility during a time period looks like. This is the basic chart before anything has been filled in. This set of charts would cover four months.

The Positions of a Time Chart

Shown below is a sample chart which shows the different positions in a time chart. Over the next pages, we will fill in a sample chart, showing how to make a chart step-by-step and position-by-position. Begin with what is called the base line, which is comprised of positions A, B, and C.

```
                    (g)
                  _____
                    (f)
                  _____
          (d)       (e)
        _____  _____
  (a)     (b)       (c)
_____ _____ _____
          (h)       (i)
        _____  _____
          (j)
        _____
       (month name)
```

Position A

Position A is filled in first—this is the month digit.

Position A is shown in the following chart. If you need to, go back and read the definition of the month digit. Position A does not change from chart to chart.

When you are making a chart, do not forget that the number for each month is reduced to its lowest numerology form (November can be either a 2 or an 11). In the following examples of how to build a chart, November will be shown as a 2, but November as an 11 can be found in the charts provided in the appendices.

(g)
_____
(f)
_____
(d)   (e)
_____   _____
(a) 1   (b)   (c)
_____ _____   _____
(h)   (i)
_____   _____
(j)
_____
January

(g)
_____
(f)
_____
(d)   (e)
_____   _____
(a) 2   (b)   (c)
_____ _____   _____
(h)   (i)
_____   _____
(j)
_____
February

(g)
_____
(f)
_____
(d)   (e)
_____   _____
(a) 3   (b)   (c)
_____ _____   _____
(h)   (i)
_____   _____
(j)
_____
March

(g)
_____
(f)
_____
(d)   (e)
_____   _____
(a) 4   (b)   (c)
_____ _____   _____
(h)   (i)
_____   _____
(j)
_____
April

a   month digit

(g)
(f)
(d)   (e)
(a) 5   (b)   (c)
(h)   (i)
(j)
May

(g)
(f)
(d)   (e)
(a) 6   (b)   (c)
(h)   (i)
(j)
June

(g)
(f)
(d)   (e)
(a) 7   (b)   (c)
(h)   (i)
(j)
July

(g)
(f)
(d)   (e)
(a) 8   (b)   (c)
(h)   (i)
(j)
August

a   month digit

	(g)	
	(f)	
(d)		(e)
(a) 9	(b)	(c)
(h)		(i)
	(j)	

September

	(g)	
	(f)	
(d)		(e)
(a) 1	(b)	(c)
(h)		(i)
	(j)	

October

	(g)	
	(f)	
(d)		(e)
(a) 2	(b)	(c)
(h)		(i)
	(j)	

November

	(g)	
	(f)	
(d)		(e)
(a) 3	(b)	(c)
(h)		(i)
	(j)	

December

a   month digit

Position B

The next step in filling out the chart is to do the middle line, position B. This position is the personal year of the individual for whom the chart is being done. To find the personal year, add the numerology digit of the birth month and day of the individual to the universal year. The birth month and day should already be reduced as far as possible. Go back and review how to find the personal year if you need to. We will use a sample birth day and month with our sample chart. This sample will be of a person born August 14th. The chart will be for 2035.

Example—Finding the Personal Year
First, find the universal year for 2035.

$$2+0+3+5 = 10$$
$$10 = 1+0$$
$$1+0 = 1$$

The universal year for 2035 is 1.

To find the personal year, add together the universal year and month and day of the birthday of the individual.

8 (August) + 5 (14 reduced) + 1 (the universal year for 2035) = 14 (14 = 1 + 4) = 5

The personal year in 2035 for a person born August 14th is 5.

Place 5 in position B of the chart.

```
            (g)                              (g)
          ─────────                        ─────────
            (f)                              (f)
          ─────────                        ─────────
     (d)        (e)                    (d)        (e)
    ─────────────────              ─────────────────
(a) 1   (b) 5   (c)            (a) 2   (b) 5   (c)
  ─────────────────────          ─────────────────────
     (h)        (i)                    (h)        (i)
    ─────────────────              ─────────────────
            (j)                              (j)
          ─────────                        ─────────
          January                         February


            (g)                              (g)
          ─────────                        ─────────
            (f)                              (f)
          ─────────                        ─────────
     (d)        (e)                    (d)        (e)
    ─────────────────              ─────────────────
(a) 3   (b) 5   (c)            (a) 4   (b) 5   (c)
  ─────────────────────          ─────────────────────
     (h)        (i)                    (h)        (i)
    ─────────────────              ─────────────────
            (j)                              (j)
          ─────────                        ─────────
           March                            April
```

a   month digit
b   personal year

```
            (g)                              (g)
         _____                     _____
            (f)                              (f)
       _____                 _____
      (d)        (e)                  (d)        (e)
     _____    _____              _____    _____
 (a) 5    (b) 5    (c)          (a) 6    (b) 5    (c)
_____   _____
      (h)        (i)                  (h)        (i)
     _____    _____              _____    _____
            (j)                              (j)
         _____                     _____
            May                             June


            (g)                              (g)
         _____                     _____
            (f)                              (f)
       _____                 _____
      (d)        (e)                  (d)        (e)
     _____    _____              _____    _____
 (a) 7    (b) 5    (c)          (a) 8    (b) 5    (c)
_____   _____
      (h)        (i)                  (h)        (i)
     _____    _____              _____    _____
            (j)                              (j)
         _____                     _____
            July                            August
```

a   month digit
b   personal year

```
          (g)                              (g)
          (f)                              (f)
      (d)       (e)                   (d)        (e)
(a) 9    (b) 5    (c)           (a) 1    (b) 5     (c)
      (h)       (i)                   (h)        (i)
          (j)                              (j)
       September                         October


          (g)                              (g)
          (f)                              (f)
      (d)       (e)                   (d)        (e)
(a) 2    (b) 5    (c)           (a) 3    (b) 5     (c)
      (h)       (i)                   (h)        (i)
          (j)                              (j)
       November                         December
```

a   month digit
b   personal year

Position C

Position C is found next. To do this, add the month digit and the personal year together by adding position A and position B. Make sure the sum is reduced as far as possible.

	(g)	
	(f)	
(d)	(e)	
(a) 1	(b) 5	(c) 6
(h)	(i)	
	(j)	

January

	(g)	
	(f)	
(d)	(e)	
(a) 2	(b) 5	(c) 7
(h)	(i)	
	(j)	

February

	(g)	
	(f)	
(d)	(e)	
(a) 3	(b) 5	(c) 8
(h)	(i)	
	(j)	

March

	(g)	
	(f)	
(d)	(e)	
(a) 4	(b) 5	(c) 9
(h)	(i)	
	(j)	

April

a   month digit
b   personal year
c   a + b

```
         (g)                              (g)
         (f)                              (f)
     (d)     (e)                      (d)     (e)
(a) 5   (b) 5   (c) 1            (a) 6   (b) 5   (c) 11
     (h)     (i)                      (h)     (i)
         (j)                              (j)
         May                             June


         (g)                              (g)
         (f)                              (f)
     (d)     (e)                      (d)     (e)
(a) 7   (b) 5   (c) 3            (a) 8   (b) 5   (c) 4
     (h)     (i)                      (h)     (i)
         (j)                              (j)
         July                           August
```

a   month digit
b   personal year
c   a + b

```
              (g)                              (g)
              ___                              ___
              (f)                              (f)
              ___                              ___
        (d)         (e)               (d)         (e)
        ___         ___               ___         ___
(a) 9       (b) 5       (c) 5   (a) 1       (b) 5       (c) 6
___         ___         ___     ___         ___         ___
        (h)         (i)               (h)         (i)
        ___         ___               ___         ___
              (j)                              (j)
              ___                              ___
          September                        October
```

```
              (g)                              (g)
              ___                              ___
              (f)                              (f)
              ___                              ___
        (d)         (e)               (d)         (e)
        ___         ___               ___         ___
(a) 2       (b) 5       (c) 7   (a) 3       (b) 5       (c) 8
___         ___         ___     ___         ___         ___
        (h)         (i)               (h)         (i)
        ___         ___               ___         ___
              (j)                              (j)
              ___                              ___
          November                        December
```

a   month digit
b   personal year
c   a + b

Position D

Position D is the number of the vibrations of the first week of the month. The characteristics of the first week, or what can be obtained during that week, will be shown by position D. It is day one through seven and includes the seventh day. It is found by adding together position A and position B. This is adding the personal year and the month digit.

```
                (g)
         _____
                (f)
         _____
           (d) 6   (e)
        _____
  (a) 1   (b) 5   (c) 6
  _____
         (h)       (i)
        _____
               (j)
          _____
            January
```

```
                (g)
         _____
                (f)
         _____
           (d) 7   (e)
        _____
  (a) 2   (b) 5   (c) 7
  _____
         (h)       (i)
        _____
               (j)
          _____
            February
```

```
                (g)
         _____
                (f)
         _____
           (d) 8   (e)
        _____
  (a) 3   (b) 5   (c) 8
  _____
         (h)       (i)
        _____
               (j)
          _____
             March
```

```
                (g)
         _____
                (f)
         _____
           (d) 9   (e)
        _____
  (a) 4   (b) 5   (c) 9
  _____
         (h)       (i)
        _____
               (j)
          _____
             April
```

a   month digit
b   personal year
c   a + b
d   day 1 to 7

	(g)	
	(f)	
(d) 1	(e)	
(a) 5	(b) 5	(c) 1
(h)	(i)	
	(j)	
	May	

	(g)	
	(f)	
(d) 11	(e)	
(a) 6	(b) 5	(c) 11
(h)	(i)	
	(j)	
	June	

	(g)	
	(f)	
(d) 3	(e)	
(a) 7	(b) 5	(c) 3
(h)	(i)	
	(j)	
	July	

	(g)	
	(f)	
(d) 4	(e)	
(a) 8	(b) 5	(c) 4
(h)	(i)	
	(j)	
	August	

a   month digit
b   personal year
c   a + b
d   day 1 to 7

```
            (g)
            ___
            (f)
            ___
      (d) 5     (e)
      _____
 (a) 9   (b) 5   (c) 5
 _____
      (h)       (i)
      _____
            (j)
            ___
        September
```

```
            (g)
            ___
            (f)
            ___
      (d) 6     (e)
      _____
 (a) 1   (b) 5   (c) 6
 _____
      (h)       (i)
      _____
            (j)
            ___
         October
```

```
            (g)
            ___
            (f)
            ___
      (d) 7     (e)
      _____
 (a) 2   (b) 5   (c) 7
 _____
      (h)       (i)
      _____
            (j)
            ___
        November
```

```
            (g)
            ___
            (f)
            ___
      (d) 8     (e)
      _____
 (a) 3   (b) 5   (c) 8
 _____
      (h)       (i)
      _____
            (j)
            ___
        December
```

a   month digit
b   personal year
c $a + b$
d   day 1 to 7

Position E

The characteristics and vibrations of the second week, or what can be obtained during that week, is shown by position E. It is day eight through fourteen, including the fourteenth. Position E is found by adding together position B and position C.

```
              (g)
              (f)
         (d) 6  (e) 11
    (a) 1  (b) 5  (c) 6
         (h)     (i)
              (j)
           January
```

```
              (g)
              (f)
         (d) 7  (e) 3
    (a) 2  (b) 5  (c) 7
         (h)     (i)
              (j)
           February
```

```
              (g)
              (f)
         (d) 8  (e) 4
    (a) 3  (b) 5  (c) 8
         (h)     (i)
              (j)
            March
```

```
              (g)
              (f)
         (d) 9  (e) 5
    (a) 4  (b) 5  (c) 9
         (h)     (i)
              (j)
            April
```

a   month digit
b   personal year
c   a + b
d   day 1 to 7
e   day 8 to 14

$\dfrac{(g)}{}$

$\dfrac{(f)}{}$

(d) 1   (e) 6

(a) 5   (b) 5   (c) 1

(h)   (i)

(j)

May

$\dfrac{(g)}{}$

$\dfrac{(f)}{}$

(d) 11   (e) 11,5

(a) 6   (b) 5   (c) 11

(h)   (i)

(j)

June

$\dfrac{(g)}{}$

$\dfrac{(f)}{}$

(d) 3   (e) 8

(a) 7   (b) 5   (c) 3

(h)   (i)

(j)

July

$\dfrac{(g)}{}$

$\dfrac{(f)}{}$

(d) 4   (e) 9

(a) 8   (b) 5   (c) 4

(h)   (i)

(j)

August

a   month digit
b   personal year
c   a + b
d   day 1 to 7
e   day 8 to 14

(g)
_____
(f)
_____
(d) 5   (e) 1
_____
(a) 9   (b) 5   (c) 5
_____
(h)   (i)
_____
(j)
_____
September

(g)
_____
(f)
_____
(d) 6   (e) 11
_____
(a) 1   (b) 5   (c) 6
_____
(h)   (i)
_____
(j)
_____
October

(g)
_____
(f)
_____
(d) 7   (e) 3
_____
(a) 2   (b) 5   (c) 7
_____
(h)   (i)
_____
(j)
_____
November

(g)
_____
(f)
_____
(d) 8   (e) 4
_____
(a) 3   (b) 5   (c) 8
_____
(h)   (i)
_____
(j)
_____
December

a   month digit
b   personal year
c   a + b
d   day 1 to 7
e   day 8 to 14

Position F

Position F shows the vibrations of the third week of the month. The characteristics of the third week of the month or what can be obtained during that week is shown by position F. It is day fifteen through twenty-one and includes the twenty-first. To find position F add together position D and position E (the first and second weeks).

(g)
_____
(f) 11,6
_____
(d) 6   (e) 11
_____
(a) 1   (b) 5   (c) 6
_____
(h)   (i)
_____
(j)
_____
January

(g)
_____
(f) 1
_____
(d) 7   (e) 3
_____
(a) 2   (b) 5   (c) 7
_____
(h)   (i)
_____
(j)
_____
February

(g)
_____
(f) 3
_____
(d) 8   (e) 4
_____
(a) 3   (b) 5   (c) 8
_____
(h)   (i)
_____
(j)
_____
March

(g)
_____
(f) 5
_____
(d) 9   (e) 5
_____
(a) 4   (b) 5   (c) 9
_____
(h)   (i)
_____
(j)
_____
April

```
        (g)
      ─────────
        (f) 7
    (d) 1   (e) 6
 (a) 5   (b) 5   (c) 1
    (h)       (i)
        (j)
        May
```

```
        (g)
      ─────────
        (f) 22,5
    (d) 11   (e) 11,5
 (a) 6   (b) 5   (c) 11
    (h)       (i)
        (j)
        June
```

```
        (g)
      ─────────
        (f) 11
    (d) 3   (e) 8
 (a) 7   (b) 5   (c) 3
    (h)       (i)
        (j)
        July
```

```
        (g)
      ─────────
        (f) 4
    (d) 4   (e) 9
 (a) 8   (b) 5   (c) 4
    (h)       (i)
        (j)
        August
```

a   month digit
b   personal year
c   a + b
d   day 1 to 7
e   day 8 to 14

f   day 15 to 21

```
                (g)
              ─────────
               (f) 6
        (d) 5      (e) 1
    (a) 9   (b) 5      (c) 5
        (h)        (i)
              ─────────
                (j)
              ─────────
              September
```

```
                (g)
              ─────────
               (f)11,6
        (d) 6      (e) 11
    (a) 1   (b) 5      (c) 6
        (h)        (i)
              ─────────
                (j)
              ─────────
               October
```

```
                (g)
              ─────────
               (f) 1
        (d) 7      (e) 3
    (a) 2   (b) 5      (c) 7
        (h)        (i)
              ─────────
                (j)
              ─────────
              November
```

```
                (g)
              ─────────
               (f) 3
        (d) 8      (e) 4
    (a) 3   (b) 5      (c) 8
        (h)        (i)
              ─────────
                (j)
              ─────────
              December
```

a   month digit   f   day 15 to 21
b   personal year
c   a + b
d   day 1 to 7
e   day 8 to 14

Position G

The vibrations of the twenty-second to the end of the month are shown by position G. It will be a little over a week, except during the month of February. The characteristics of this time period and what can be obtained will be shown by this position. Position G is found by adding together position A and C.

```
        (g) 7                           (g) 9
        ─────                           ─────
        (f)11,6                         (f) 1
        ───────                         ─────
      (d) 6   (e) 11                  (d) 7   (e) 3
      ─────   ──────                  ─────   ─────
(a) 1   (b) 5   (c) 6           (a) 2   (b) 5   (c) 7
        ─────   ──────                  ─────   ──────
      (h)     (i)                     (h)     (i)
      ─────   ─────                   ─────   ─────
        (j)                             (j)
        ─────                           ─────
      January                         February
```

```
        (g) 11                          (g) 4
        ──────                          ─────
        (f) 3                           (f) 5
        ─────                           ─────
      (d) 8   (e) 4                   (d) 9   (e) 5
      ─────   ─────                   ─────   ─────
(a) 3   (b) 5   (c) 8           (a) 4   (b) 5   (c) 9
        ─────   ─────                   ─────   ─────
      (h)     (i)                     (h)     (i)
      ─────   ─────                   ─────   ─────
        (j)                             (j)
        ─────                           ─────
       March                           April
```

a   month digit
b   personal year
c   a + b
d   day 1 to 7
e   day 8 to 14

f   day 15 to 21
g   day 22 to month's end

(g) 6
(f) 7
(d) 1   (e) 6
(a) 5   (b) 5   (c) 1
(h)   (i)
(j)
May

(g) 11,6
(f) 22,5
(d) 11   (e) 11,5
(a) 6   (b) 5   (c) 11
(h)   (i)
(j)
June

(g) 1
(f) 11
(d) 3   (e) 8
(a) 7   (b) 5   (c) 3
(h)   (i)
(j)
July

(g) 3
(f) 4
(d) 4   (e) 9
(a) 8   (b) 5   (c) 4
(h)   (i)
(j)
August

a   month digit
b   personal year
c   a + b
d   day 1 to 7
e   day 8 to 14
f   day 15 to 21
g   day 22 to month's end

(g) 5
―――――
(f) 6
―――――
(d) 5   (e) 1
―――――――――
(a) 9   (b) 5   (c) 5
―――――――――――
(h)   (i)
―――――――――
(j)
―――――
September

(g) 7
―――――
(f)11,6
―――――
(d) 6   (e) 11
―――――――――
(a) 1   (b) 5   (c) 6
―――――――――――
(h)   (i)
―――――――――
(j)
―――――
October

(g) 9
―――――
(f) 1
―――――
(d) 7   (e) 3
―――――――――
(a) 2   (b) 5   (c) 7
―――――――――――
(h)   (i)
―――――――――
(j)
―――――
November

(g) 11
―――――
(f) 3
―――――
(d) 8   (e) 4
―――――――――
(a) 3   (b) 5   (c) 8
―――――――――――
(h)   (i)
―――――――――
(j)
―――――
December

a   month digit
b   personal year
c   a + b
d   day 1 to 7
e   day 8 to 14

f   day 15 to 21
g   day 22 to month's end

The Attainments

The attainments is the name given to the bottom part of the numerology chart for finding compatibility. The attainments are found in a manner different from the top part of the chart. Instead of addition, subtraction is used. This is a case where master numbers are reduced to their lower vibration for clarity. For example, an 11 would be read as a 2. Follow the steps for doing this, one by one, to see how each position is obtained.

Position H

There are usually one major and two minor attainments for each month. Position H shows the first minor attainment, which is found by subtracting position A and position B. Remember to always subtract the smaller number from the larger number.

```
              (g) 7                          (g) 9
             (f) 11,6                        (f) 1
        (d) 6   (e) 11                   (d) 7   (e) 3
   (a) 1   (b) 5   (c) 6           (a) 2   (b) 5   (c) 7
        (h) 4   (i)                     (h) 3   (i)
             (j)                             (j)
          January                         February
```

```
            (g) 11                            (g) 4
            ─────                             ────
            (f) 3                             (f) 5
      ─────────────                     ─────────────
      (d) 8   (e) 4                     (d) 9   (e) 5
────────────────────────         ────────────────────────
(a) 3   (b) 5   (c) 8             (a) 4   (b) 5   (c) 9
      ─────────────                     ─────────────
      (h) 2   (i)                       (h) 1   (i)
      ─────────────                     ─────────────
            (j)                               (j)
           March                             April
```

```
            (g) 6                            (g)11,6
            ─────                            ──────
            (f) 7                            (f) 22,5
      ─────────────                     ───────────────
      (d) 1   (e) 6                     (d) 11  (e)11,5
────────────────────────         ────────────────────────
(a) 5   (b) 5   (c) 1             (a) 6   (b) 5   (c) 11
      ─────────────                     ─────────────
      (h) 0   (i)                       (h) 1   (i)
      ─────────────                     ─────────────
            (j)                               (j)
            May                             June
```

a   month digit
b   personal year
c   a + b
d   day 1 to 7
e   day 8 to 14

f   day 15 to 21
g   day 22 to month's end
h   minor attainment

```
            (g) 1                              (g) 3
           _____                           _____
            (f) 11                             (f) 4
           _____                           _____
      (d) 3     (e) 8                    (d) 4     (e) 9
     _____  _____                 _____  _____
(a) 7     (b) 5     (c) 3          (a) 8     (b) 5     (c) 4
_____  _____  _____       _____  _____  _____
      (h) 2     (i)                     (h) 3     (i)
     _____  _____                 _____  _____
            (j)                              (j)
           _____                          _____
            July                             August
```

```
            (g) 5                              (g) 7
           _____                           _____
            (f) 6                             (f)11,6
           _____                           _____
      (d) 5     (e) 1                    (d) 6     (e) 11
     _____  _____                 _____  _____
(a) 9     (b) 5     (c) 5          (a) 1     (b) 5     (c) 6
_____  _____  _____       _____  _____  _____
      (h) 4     (i)                     (h) 4     (i)
     _____  _____                 _____  _____
            (j)                              (j)
           _____                          _____
         September                          October
```

a   month digit
b   personal year
c   a + b
d   day 1 to 7
e   day 8 to 14

f   day 15 to 21
g   day 22 to month's end
h   minor attainment

$$\frac{\text{(g) 9}}{}$$
$$\frac{\text{(f) 1}}{}$$

(d) 7 ___ (e) 3

(a) 2 ___ (b) 5 ___ (c) 7

(h) 3 ___ (i)

(j) ___

November

$$\frac{\text{(g) 11}}{}$$
$$\frac{\text{(f) 3}}{}$$

(d) 8 ___ (e) 4

(a) 3 ___ (b) 5 ___ (c) 8

(h) 2 ___ (i)

(j) ___

December

Position I

The second minor attainment for the month is position I. To find position I, subtract position B and position C. Subtract the smaller number from the larger number. If either position B or position C is a master number, reduce the master number to its lower vibration before subtracting.

$$\frac{\text{(g) 7}}{}$$
$$\frac{\text{(f) 11,6}}{}$$

(d) 6 ___ (e) 11

(a) 1 ___ (b) 5 ___ (c) 6

(h) 4 ___ (i) 1

(j) ___

January

$$\frac{\text{(g) 9}}{}$$
$$\frac{\text{(f) 1}}{}$$

(d) 7 ___ (e) 3

(a) 2 ___ (b) 5 ___ (c) 7

(h) 3 ___ (i) 2

(j) ___

February

	(g) 11	
	(f) 3	
(d) 8	(e) 4	
(a) 3	(b) 5	(c) 8
(h) 2	(i) 3	
	(j)	
	March	

	(g) 4	
	(f) 5	
(d) 9	(e) 5	
(a) 4	(b) 5	(c) 9
(h) 1	(i) 4	
	(j)	
	April	

	(g) 6	
	(f) 7	
(d) 1	(e) 6	
(a) 5	(b) 5	(c) 1
(h) 0	(i) 4	
	(j)	
	May	

	(g)11,6	
	(f)22,5	
(d) 11	(e)11,5	
(a) 6	(b) 5	(c) 11
(h) 1	(i) 3	
	(j)	
	June	

a	month digit	f	day 15 to 21
b	personal year	g	day 22 to month's end
c	a + b	h	minor attainment
d	day 1 to 7	i	minor attainment
e	day 8 to 14		

	(g) 1	
	(f) 11	
(d) 3	(e) 8	
(a) 7 (b) 5	(c) 3	
(h) 2	(i) 2	
	(j)	
	July	

	(g) 3	
	(f) 4	
(d) 4	(e) 9	
(a) 8 (b) 5	(c) 4	
(h) 3	(i) 1	
	(j)	
	August	

	(g) 5	
	(f) 6	
(d) 5	(e) 1	
(a) 9 (b) 5	(c) 5	
(h) 4	(i) 0	
	(j)	
	September	

	(g) 7	
	(f)11,6	
(d) 6	(e) 11	
(a) 1 (b) 5	(c) 6	
(h) 4	(i) 1	
	(j)	
	October	

a   month digit
b   personal year
c   a + b
d   day 1 to 7
e   day 8 to 14

f   day 15 to 21
g   day 22 to month's end
h   minor attainment
i   minor attainment

	(g) 9				(g) 11	
	(f) 1				(f) 3	
(d) 7	(e) 3			(d) 8	(e) 4	
(a) 2	(b) 5	(c) 7		(a) 3	(b) 5	(c) 8
	(h) 3	(i) 2			(h) 2	(i) 3
	(j)				(j)	
	November				December	

Position J

The major attainment for the month is position J. Position J is found by subtracting position H and position I—the two minor attainments. Subtract whichever is smaller from the larger. If position H or position I is a master number, reduce the master number to its lower vibration before subtracting.

	(g) 7				(g) 9	
	(f) 11,6				(f) 1	
(d) 6	(e) 11			(d) 7	(e) 3	
(a) 1	(b) 5	(c) 6		(a) 2	(b) 5	(c) 7
	(h) 4	(i) 1			(h) 3	(i) 2
	(j) 3				(j) 1	
	January				February	

	(g) 11	
	(f) 3	
(d) 8	(e) 4	
(a) 3	(b) 5	(c) 8
(h) 2	(i) 3	
	(j) 1	

March

	(g) 4	
	(f) 5	
(d) 9	(e) 5	
(a) 4	(b) 5·	(c) 9
(h) 1	(i) 4	
	(j) 3	

April

	(g) 6	
	(f) 7	
(d) 1	(e) 6	
(a) 5	(b) 5	(c) 1
(h) 0	(i) 4	
	(j) 4	

May

	(g) 11,6	
	(f) 22,5	
(d) 11	(e) 11,5	
(a) 6	(b) 5	(c) 11
(h) 1	(i) 3	
	(j) 2	

June

a month digit	f day 15 to 21
b personal year	g day 22 to month's end
c a + b	h minor attainment
d day 1 to 7	i minor attainment
e day 8 to 14	j major attainment

	(g) 1	
	(f) 11	
(d) 3		(e) 8
(a) 7	(b) 5	(c) 3
	(h) 2	(i) 2
	(j) 0	

July

	(g) 3	
	(f) 4	
(d) 4		(e) 9
(a) 8	(b) 5	(c) 4
	(h) 3	(i) 1
	(j) 2	

August

	(g) 5	
	(f) 6	
(d) 5		(e) 1
(a) 9	(b) 5	(c) 5
	(h) 4	(i) 0
	(j) 4	

September

	(g) 7	
	(f) 11,6	
(d) 6		(e) 11
(a) 1	(b) 5	(c) 6
	(h) 4	(i) 1
	(j) 3	

October

a	month digit	f	day 15 to 21
b	personal year	g	day 22 to month's end
c	a + b	h	minor attainment
d	day 1 to 7	i	minor attainment
e	day 8 to 14	j	major attainment

$$
\begin{array}{c}
\overline{\text{(g) 9}} \\
\overline{\text{(f) 1}} \\
\overline{\text{(d) 7} \quad \text{(e) 3}} \\
\text{(a) 2} \quad \text{(b) 5} \quad \text{(c) 7} \\
\overline{\text{(h) 3} \quad \text{(i) 2}} \\
\overline{\text{(j) 1}}
\end{array}
$$

November

$$
\begin{array}{c}
\overline{\text{(g) 11}} \\
\overline{\text{(f) 3}} \\
\overline{\text{(d) 8} \quad \text{(e) 4}} \\
\text{(a) 3} \quad \text{(b) 5} \quad \text{(c) 8} \\
\overline{\text{(h) 2} \quad \text{(i) 3}} \\
\overline{\text{(j) 1}}
\end{array}
$$

December

a   month digit
b   personal year
c   a + b
d   day 1 to 7
e   day 8 to 14
f   day 15 to 21
g   day 22 to month's end
h   minor attainment
i   minor attainment
j   major attainment

Chapter Seven

Characteristics of the Vibrations of Time

In the previous chapter, a time chart was constructed. The next step in using time vibrations is to learn the characteristics of each time period. Certain time periods are better than others for seeking compatibility. Both a knowledge of innate vibrational compatibility and compatibility by time period are necessary for a complete understanding of how to use vibrations to determine compatibility. The following list will show how you can expect to feel during each time period and how the time period affects compatibility.

The Main Nine Numbers

1 as a Vibration of Time

During a 1 period, it is a time to stand alone. It is not a good time for reaching out or seeking companionship. The 1, as a vibration of a time period, will produce just what it implies, a time of being alone. This does not mean that you cannot seek companionship under a 1, but it will be found over and over that you are often alone at this time. It is also a time when selfishness and impatience tend to be greater than usual, as these are characteristics of the 1.

2 as a Vibration of Time

The 2 is a time that is good for companionship and joining with others. It is a quiet time when the personal ego is gentle and you are more responsive to the needs of others. It is one of the gentlest of vibrations, it brings people together, it and can produce love because it makes them want to be with others. The gentleness and kindness associated with a 2 make it good for seeking compatibility.

3 as a Vibration of Time

The 3 is a good time for making friendships, as it is a social time. You will usually be in a light, friendly mood under the 3. You may be more talkative and outgoing than usual. The 3 is a good time for going out and making new friends, and going to parties, dinners, or on outings.

4 as a Vibration of Time

The 4 is not a good time to look for compatibility. The 4 tends to relate mostly to work. It tends to be limiting and can be harsh. Under the 4, you must be careful not to lose what could have been compatibility under another vibration. Sometimes, you will come together with those whom you are innately compatible with under the 4 and lose a chance for the affection from the innate compatibility to grow.

5 as a Vibration of Time

The 5 in relationship to compatibility can be either positive or negative—it depends on the type of compatibility you are seeking. The 5 is the vibration that makes the sexes attract. It helps with initial attractions and establishing sexual compatibility. This can be both good and bad. If you are attracted to someone who has innate vibrations that are compatible, then the 5 is useful for establishing long-term relationships. If the 5 brings you together with someone who is not really innately compatible, then the relationship will probably not last. This is the cause of many relationships being just temporary. However, the 5 is a good time to get out and try to find compatibility.

6 as a Vibration of Time

The 6 is a time that is one of the best for seeking compatibility and, if positive, can bring love. It is one of the best for producing love. It can be love whether or not the person you are attracted to has innate vibrations that are compatible. If your vibrations and those of the other person are not innately compatible, you may have a loving feeling while under the 6—but that feeling could, and probably will, fade when the 6 is gone. Under the positive 6, you and others will appear prettier and may act kinder than usual. This will enhance the loving feeling. If you or others are negative, then the great benefit of the 6 will be missed. Argumentativeness and jealousy may arise, instead of a loving feeling.

7 as a Vibration of Time

The 7 is a period of time that is not really good for seeking compatibility. If the 7 is combined with other vibrations this may be different, but a simple 7 is a vibration when you will like to be alone. Another characteristic that makes the 7 not a very good time to look for compatibility is that under the 7 things have to happen by chance and come unexpectedly. When seeking companionship under the 7, the best approach might be to reach out—even when and where you feel that you will not be accepted and where you feel compatibility will not grow.

8 as a Vibration of Time

The 8 is a period of time that really is not very good for seeking compatibility, unless the 8 is combined with another vibration that is good for seeking compatibility. The 8 is basically a materialistic vibration, making it useful for material pursuits. In terms of compatibility in a time period, the 8 as a simple 8 is not the best time to seek compatibility.

9 as a Vibration of Time

The 9, as a vibration of a time period, is a good time to seek compatibility. The compatibility found under a 9 may be more universal than personal, but that does not mean that it is not a good time to start friendships or relationships. The 9 appeals to humanity in general, and is a very giving vibration.

The Master Numbers

11 as a Vibration of Time

The 11, as a vibration of a time period, indicates a good time to seek companionship. The 11 is the higher vibration of the 2 and has the characteristics of being a good number to form partnerships, find companionship, or to seek friendships. The 11 tends to be an intuitive time, so that may help in knowing who to seek for compatibility. The 11 also tends to give appeal to your personality, which would help in seeking compatibility.

22 as a Vibration of Time

The 22, as a vibration of time, is sometimes good for seeking compatibility, but sometimes not. It depends on how the 22 is being lived. If the 22 is being lived as a 4, then it is not a good time for seeking compatibility, because the 4 tends to be a limiting, harsh number. It is not a social number. If the 22 is being lived as a 22, then it may be a good time to reach out—but it may be on a more general level then on a personal level. The 22 tends to reach out to humanity rather than for personal companionship.

33 as a Vibration of Time

As a vibration of time, the 33 is a very good time for seeking compatibility, because the 33 is the higher vibration of the 6, one of best vibrations for seeking compatibility. The 33 also has within it the element of the 11 and the 3. Both the 11 and the 3 are vibrations that can bring out friendliness and a desire to be with others. This is not a time to let pass by in a search for compatibility, but be aware of the fact that the innate vibrations should be compatible first, or the relationship will probably be temporary. The 33 is rather rare as a vibration of time and will show up as a compound number.

44 as a Vibration of Time

The 44, as a vibration of time, is definitely not a good time to seek compatibility. At this time, even with those with whom your innate compatibility may be high, you may have problems. This is because the 44 has within it the elements of the 8 and the 4. These are two very material vibrations and should be left for that purpose. If negative, the 4 can be very detrimental to seeking compatibility. Your reaction may be dislike of the other person, even in cases of high innate compatibility. It is better to wait for this time period to pass. The 44 is a rare vibration of time and will show up as a compound number.

55 as a Vibration of Time

The 55, as a vibration of time, is a good time to seek compatibility in some ways. The 55 is a form of the 1, which is not a good time to seek compatibility. However, the 55 has within it an intensified 5 vibration. The 5 can be a good time to seek compatibility because the 5 is the vibration that helps men and women attract each other. The 5 works like a magnet in this function. Also within the 55 is the 11, which is a vibration that makes you like to join with others. The overall 1 and the 11 are often opposite elements within the same compound. The 55 is a rare vibration as a vibration of time and will be found as a compound number.

66 as a Vibration of Time

The 66, as a vibration of time, is one of the best times to seek compatibility, friendship, or love. The 66 has within it the elements of the 11, the 6, and the 3. All these vibrations are good for reaching out to others for compatibility, friendship, or love. This is not a time to let pass by. The 66 is a rare vibration of time and will be a compound number.

77 as a Vibration of Time

The 77, as a vibration of time, may or may not be a good time to seek compatibility. This vibration has conflicting elements in it. It has within it the 7, which is not at all a good time to seek compatibility as it makes you like to be alone and makes things have to happen unexpectedly. However, the 77 also has the elements of the 11 and the overall vibration of the 5, both of which are good for seeking compatibility. The 77 is a very rare vibrational possibility. When it is found, it will be as a compound number.

88 as a Vibration of Time

The 88, as a vibration of time, is not a good time to seek compatibility. The 88 is a form of the 7 and has within it the element of the 8, neither of which are good for seeking compatibility. It does have the element of the 11, which changes it to be a little better in the search for compatibility, but that 11 is just one element, whereas the overall vibration is still 7. This is a very rare vibration in a numerology chart of time. It only shows up in November of a 22 year in the form of 22,22,22,11,11—a compound number.

99 as a Vibration of Time

The 99, as a vibration of time, would be extremely rare, but could happen if the personal year is a compound number. If this vibration does occur, it is a very good time to look for compatibility because the 99 has within it the elements of the 11 and the 9, making it a very good time. The 9 and 11 are very social and giving vibrations.

Compound Numbers

Often, compound numbers will be found in a time chart. This happens for different reasons. The month of November, which equals an 11, is one reason. Other reasons may be that the month digit and personal year add up to a master number or the personal year, itself, is a master number. In this section, the compound numbers that show up most frequently will be discussed.

11,1 as a Vibration of Time

The 11,1, as a vibration of a time period, may or may not be a good time to seek compatibility. It depends on the part of the compound that is dominating—and this will usually change back and forth. Sometimes, part of the compound will dominate, and sometimes it will be the overall value of the compound that is dominating. In the case of an 11,1, if the 1 is dominant, it is not a good time to seek compatibility. If it is the 11 that is dominant, then it is a good time to seek compatibility. If the 3 is dominant (the overall characteristic of an 11,1), then it is a good time to seek compatibility, most likely in friendship.

11,2 as a Vibration of Time

The 11,2 as a vibration of a time period, may or may not be a good time to seek compatibility. If the 11 or 2 is dominant then there will be a seeking to be with others, however, the overall characteristics of the 11,2 is the 4, which is not a good time for seeking compatibility. The 4 is a time to pay attention to work. This vibration could be used creatively to seek companionship within a work context, or maybe you could work with another to seek companionship at this time.

11,3 as a Vibration of Time

The 11,3, as a vibration of a time period, is a very good time to seek friendship. The 11,3 has the elements of the 3, which seeks friendship, and the 11, which is a number for seeking togetherness. The overall characteristic of the 11,3 is the 5. This, too, indicates a good time for seeking companionship. The 5 is a very social vibration and one that draws individuals together. The 11 tends to make your personality stand out more as well, so this would help in the building of relationships. The 11,3 is a very good time to seek compatibility.

11,4 as a Vibration of Time

The 11,4, as a vibration of a time period, will usually be a good time to seek compatibility, but it will depend on which part of the 11,4 is dominating, or if the overall 6 is dominating. If the 4 is dominating, then this is not a good time to seek compatibility. If the 11 or 6 is dominant, then it is a good time. This is a vibration during which it would be wise to use creativity. Compatibility could be found by working with someone else—maybe working within the areas that a 6 or 11 have an interest in.

11,5 as a Vibration of Time

The 11,5, as a vibration of a time period, has the possibility of being a good time to look for compatibility. The 11,5 is a form of the 7, so things must happen by chance or unexpectedly. The 7 makes you like to be alone, but the 11 makes you like to join with others. The 5 brings a want of social activities.

There are contradictory urges under the 11,5. If you are seeking compatibility, the best way to handle it under the 11,5 is to try even though the 7 may make you feel like doing otherwise. The 11 and 5 coupled together are a good combination for initial attraction between individuals. However, look at any vibration according to the type of compatibility that is being sought. The 5 could also bring friendship, especially since it brings social occasions and activity.

The 5 has the characteristic of changing interests often, of moving from interest to interest, so the 5 could bring short-term friendships, short-term compatibility, or short-term love. This is where you really need to know the difference between innate vibrations and vibrations of a time period.

11,6 as a Vibration of Time

The 11,6, as a vibration of a time period, can be a good time to look for compatibility. This is because it is a compound made up of both the 11 and 6. The 11,6 is a form of the 8, which will also influence what happens at this time. The influence of the 8 could bring in the aspect of the material, something about money, or about work.

Sometimes the 8 influence will be a descriptor of the type of 6 and 11 influence. For example, the 6 might bring love, and the 8 could give the vibration for it to be a rich person to love. With the 11 and 6 together, you might find someone who is very attractive—as both the 11 and 6 can give added beauty and attraction.

The main value of this compound for finding compatibility or love is that both the 6 and 11 are present. The 6 and 11 are main numbers for producing love.

11,7 as a Vibration of Time

The 11,7, as a vibration of a time period, may or may not be a good time for seeking compatibility. The 7 in this compound means that if compatibility is to be found at this time, it must come by chance. Under the 11,7, there is a contradiction for looking for compatibility. The 7 makes you like to be alone, but the 11 will make you want to seek out others. The 9, as the overall characteristic of this compound, will give you the urge to seek out others. If you are seeking compatibility, the best approach under the 11,7 may be just to try, even if the 7 makes you feel like not doing so.

11,8 as a Vibration of Time

The 11,8, as a vibration of a time period, is not a good time to seek compatibility. It does have the 11, which is a good vibration for compatibility, but the overall vibration is a 1, which is not a good time. The characteristics of the 8 are also present, which is not a good time for looking for compatibility either. The 11,8 is mostly a time for self and for material pursuits, even though it is a softened 1 with the characteristics of the 11 present.

11,9 as a Vibration of Time

The 11,9 vibration indicates a very good time to seek compatibility. This compound is made up of two good vibrations for seeking compatibility—the 11 and the 9. The overall vibration of a 2 is also good. This is not a time to let go by when you are seeking compatibility. The 11 and 9 may bring in a wider loving feeling than just personal love, because the 11 is often religious and the 9 reaches out to humanity. Still, personal compatibility could be found during this time. It is the 6th vibration that brings a more personal love. Under the 11 and 9, the greater, wider side of your personality might come through, thus also producing love.

11,11 as a Vibration of Time

The 11,11, as a vibration of a time period, may or may not be a good time to seek compatibility. This is because the 11 is a good time to seek compatibility, but the overall vibration can be the 4, which is not a good time to seek compatibility, friendship, or love. Whether or not this is a good time to seek will depend on if the characteristics of the 11, the 22, or the 4 are dominant. If the 11 or 22 is dominant, then it is a good time to seek compatibility. If the 4 is dominant, then it is not a good time to seek.

11,22 as a Vibration of Time

The 11,22, as a vibration of a time period, is a very good time to seek compatibility, friendship, or love. The overall vibration of the 11,22 is 6, which is a very loving vibration. Also, the two vibrations that make up this compound, the 11 and the 22, are both very loving.

A sense of knowing what to do, added confidence, added intuition, and the ability to see things as they really are, will be present under a positive 11,22. This is not a time to let go by. There is so much potential good feeling and giving with this compound.

When you are under this compound, you will probably be more careful about your appearance and will look very good to others.

22,1 as a Vibration of Time

In a numerology chart of time in relationship to compatibility, the number 22 will be rare. The 22,1 is a form of the 5, but it also has within it the influence of the 22, 4, 2, 1, and sometimes 11. This may or may not be a good time to seek compatibility, depending on the part of the compound that is dominant. If the 22, 11, 5, or 2 is dominant then this will be a time to seek compatibility. If the 4 or 1 is dominant, then it is not a good time. When you are under this vibration, you can usually tell which part of the vibration is dominant. Actually, you are in control and it is up to you which part of a compound is allowed to dominate.

The 22 and the 1 of this compound can cause you to be too domineering of others, as both of these numbers tend to dominate. This may be a hindrance to forming relationships and seeking compatibility. On the other hand, the overall 5 of the 22,1 compound will tend to make you very social and seek good times, which would enhance the seeking of compatibility. This is a time period that should be analyzed very closely to determine what is really going on.

22,2 as a Vibration of Time

The 22,2 is a form of the 6, so it has the elements of the 6, as well as influences of the 22, 4, 2, and sometimes the 11. The 22,2 is a very good time to look for compatibility, because of the influence of the 22, 11, 6, and 2. The 22,2 is a vibration that will bring a strong urge to be with others. All four vibrations, the overall 6, the 22, the 11, and the 2 are vibrations that make you want to be with others.

The 6 is the vibration of personal love. The 22 is the vibration of a love of humanity. The 11 is the vibration of a love of God. The 2 is a vibration that brings a desire to be with and do for others. The 22,2 time is a very good time to look for compatibility or love.

22,3 as a Vibration of Time

The 22,3 is a form of the 7, so it has within it the elements of the 7, 22, 4, 3, and sometimes the 11. It may or may not be a good time to look for compatibility.

With the element of the 7, things will have to come to you by chance. This includes compatibility, friendship, and love. The 7 is also a vibration that tends to make you want to be alone, so that urge may hold you back from finding compatibility.

The 22,3, however, is not a simple 7. It is made up of two vibrations that do give you the urge to be with others—the 22 and 3. Under the 22,3, you will be much more social than under a simple 7. It should be a quiet but friendly time.

22,4 as a Vibration of Time

The 22,4 is a form of the 8, but it has within it the influence of the 22, the 4, the 2, and sometimes the 11. This compound will bring a time period that is chiefly materially oriented because the overall 8, the 22, and the 4 all have strong material influences. The 4 will also make this time rather hard and not always loving. The 22, the 11, and the 2 influences will bring some wish to be with others, but the overall 8 and materialistic influences of the 22 and 4 will probably override the good of the social influences in this compound. This is a time when it is probably best to seek something other than compatibility.

22,5 as a Vibration of Time

The 22,5 is a form of the 9, so it has within it the characteristics of the 9 and the influence of the 22, the 5, the 4, the 2, and sometimes the 11. All the elements of this compound, except for the 4, make it a good vibration for seeking compatibility. Both the 22 and 9, are very humanity oriented and the 5 likes good times. It is a good time to get out with others and seek compatibility. The 22,5 may make this time period less personal than other good times for compatibility, because both the 22, and overall 9 are loving, but that love is a wider love of humanity. It would still be a good time to get out and try, though.

22,6 as a Vibration of Time

The 22,6 is a form of the 1, so it has the characteristics of the 1 as well as those of the 22, 6, 4, 2 and sometimes the 11. This can be a good time to look for compatibility, though not always.

The overall 1 makes this a poor time to seek others, because the one is the vibration of self, of ego, and of standing alone. The elements of the 22, 11, 6, and 2 are all opposite to the vibration of the 1, however. They are vibrations that bring the urge to give to others. Because of these opposite vibrations, there will probably be a lot of contradictions under this vibration. It is a good idea to get out and try during this time.

22,7 as a Vibration of Time

The 22,7 is a form of the 11, but it has within it the elements of the 22, 11, 7, 4, and 2. This is a time that may or may not be a good time to seek compatibility since it has conflicting elements, as many compounds do.

The 7 will make it so things have to happen by chance, and you will also tend to like to be alone during the 7. However, the overall 11, the 22, and the 2 elements of this compound will influence you to enjoy being with others. Most likely, you will go back and forth between the elements of this compound. Quiet activities might be good during this time.

22,8 as a Vibration of Time

The 22,8 is a form of the 3, and also has within it the characteristics of the 22, 8, 4, 2, and sometimes 11. The 22,8 may or may not be a good time to look for compatibility. The overall 3, the 22, the 11, and the 2 make it a good time—but this is a very material 3, not a simple 3. The 22 is also a very material number. The overall 3 will usually make this a very friendly time, so it could be useful in looking for compatibility.

22,9 as a Vibration of Time

The 22,9 is a form of the 22 or 4, so it has the characteristics of these numbers as well as the influence of the 9, 2, and sometimes the 11. This may or may not be a good time to look for compatibility. It is a good time if the 22, 11, 9, or 2 is dominant. If the 4 is dominant, it is not. The influence of the 4 may bring a harshness to the time.

22,11 as a Vibration of Time

The 22,11 is a form of the 33, so it has the characteristics of the 33 or 6, but also the influence of the 22, 11, 4, and 2. Usually, this will be a very good time to look for compatibility because there are so many good vibrations in this compound. The overall 33 and 6 are very good for seeking compatibility as are the 22, 11, and 2. If the 4 influence is too strong, it may not be a good time to seek compatibility, but this will usually be overridden by the other vibrations. Also see the 11,22 vibration, which is the same thing.

Note: There is the possibility of even larger compound numbers in a time chart. When this happens, find the basic characteristics of the time period by looking up the elements that make up the compound number.

Chapter Eight

Other Factors to Consider for Compatibility

Besides knowing how to use numerology to understand innate compatibility, which can bring permanent compatibility, and the vibrations of time, which bring temporary compatibility, there are other factors that should be examined, to completely determine the situation. These factors are biorhythms and social factors.

You can learn to use biorhythms from books on the topic. Social factors that can help determine compatibility are so vast that you will have to evaluate them for yourself.

Using Biorhythms

This section is very important. In conjunction with numerology, a chart of biorhythms should be used to get an accurate assessment of compatibility between individuals.

Biorhythms are the physical, emotional, and mental cycles of the human body and mind.

After reading about how to use numerology to find people with compatible vibrations, you should next study biorhythms and learn how to read biorhythm charts to tell vibrational compatibility from them. Numerology can show you a large part of what causes compatibility, friendship, and love. However, to get a whole, true assessment of the compatibility between or among people, you need to combine a knowledge of numerology and biorhythms.

Biorhythm charts are not included in this book because the study of biorhythms would easily cover a book by itself. However, to find true compatibility, it is important to know the percentages of biorhythmic compatibility along with the numerology compatibility. In a biorhythm chart, you should look for the highest percentage possible in physical, emotional, and mental compatibility. A figure of over fifty percent is considered high.

The reason biorhythms are so important is that sometimes you will find people whose vibrations according to numerology match well, but with low biorhythms in a particular area—such as emotional—they will actually be irritating to one another instead of feeling good together.

Social Factors in Vibrational Compatibility

It will be found that innate vibrational compatibility, as shown by numerology, cuts across all social barriers. Social factors such as age, sex, race, social status, occupation, wealth, and beauty will of course affect compatibility. Very few people are spiritually minded enough to overlook all social factors. However, it is shown over and over again that with long-term relationships there will be innate vibrational compatibility regardless of social factors. If this innate vibrational compatibility is not present, the relationship will have problems or will not last.

This is why, when you learn to use numerology to find compatibility, you should know the difference between innate vibrational compatibility and compatibility that is only by vibrations of time. Time period vibrations change. Innate vibrations do not.

In order to find very good compatibility and love, you need to look for someone whose innate vibrations and social factors are compatible with yours. As the seeker of compatibility, you have to be the judge of what social differences—or degrees of difference—you are willing to accept or can handle.

Appendices

Sample Charts of
Personal Years

The following pages will show how each personal year should look in a numerology chart to examine compatibility, friendship, or love. When reading these charts, the attainments of each month are found by using the lower vibration of the master numbers. November is shown twice, first in the main personal year charts it is shown as a 2. Following these charts is a separate chart in which November is shown by itself as an 11.

Personal Year 1

	(g) 3	
	(f) 5	
(d) 2		(e) 3
(a) 1	(b) 1	(c) 2
	(h) 0	(i) 1
	(j) 1	
	January	

	(g) 5	
	(f) 7	
(d) 3		(e) 4
(a) 2	(b) 1	(c) 3
	(h) 1	(i) 2
	(j) 1	
	February	

	(g) 7	
	(f) 9	
(d) 4		(e) 5
(a) 3	(b) 1	(c) 4
	(h) 2	(i) 3
	(j) 1	
	March	

	(g) 9	
	(f) 11	
(d) 5		(e) 6
(a) 4	(b) 1	(c) 5
	(h) 3	(i) 4
	(j) 1	
	April	

a   month digit
b   personal year
c   a + b
d   day 1 to 7
e   day 8 to 14

f   day 15 to 21
g   day 22 to month's end
h   minor attainment
i   minor attainment
j   major attainment

		(g) 11		
		(f) 4		
	(d) 6		(e) 7	
(a) 5		(b) 1		(c) 6
	(h) 4		(i) 5	
		(j) 1		
		May		

		(g) 4		
		(f) 6		
	(d) 7		(e) 8	
(a) 6		(b) 1		(c) 7
	(h) 5		(i) 6	
		(j) 1		
		June		

		(g) 6		
		(f) 8		
	(d) 8		(e) 9	
(a) 7		(b) 1		(c) 8
	(h) 6		(i) 7	
		(j) 1		
		July		

		(g) 8		
		(f) 1		
	(d) 9		(e) 1	
(a) 8		(b) 1		(c) 9
	(h) 7		(i) 8	
		(j) 1		
		August		

a	month digit		f	day 15 to 21
b	personal year		g	day 22 to month's end
c	a + b		h	minor attainment
d	day 1 to 7		i	minor attainment
e	day 8 to 14		j	major attainment

210

```
        (g) 1
        (f) 3
   (d) 1    (e) 2
(a) 9  (b) 1   (c) 1
    (h) 8  (i) 0
        (j) 8
      September
```

```
        (g) 3
        (f) 5
   (d) 2    (e) 3
(a) 1  (b) 1   (c) 2
    (h) 0  (i) 1
        (j) 1
       October
```

```
        (g) 5
        (f) 7
   (d) 3    (e) 4
(a) 2  (b) 1   (c) 3
    (h) 1  (i) 2
        (j) 1
      November
```

```
        (g) 7
        (f) 9
   (d) 4    (e) 5
(a) 3  (b) 1   (c) 4
    (h) 2  (i) 3
        (j) 1
      December
```

a	month digit	f	day 15 to 21
b	personal year	g	day 22 to month's end
c	a + b	h	minor attainment
d	day 1 to 7	i	minor attainment
e	day 8 to 14	j	major attainment

Personal Year 2

	(g) 4	
	(f) 8	
	(d) 3	(e) 5
(a) 1	(b) 2	(c) 3
	(h) 1	(i) 1
	(j) 0	

January

	(g) 6	
	(f) 1	
	(d) 4	(e) 6
(a) 2	(b) 2	(c) 4
	(h) 0	(i) 2
	(j) 2	

February

	(g) 8	
	(f) 3	
	(d) 5	(e) 7
(a) 3	(b) 2	(c) 5
	(h) 1	(i) 3
	(j) 2	

March

	(g) 1	
	(f) 5	
	(d) 6	(e) 8
(a) 4	(b) 2	(c) 6
	(h) 2	(i) 4
	(j) 2	

April

a   month digit
b   personal year
c   a + b
d   day 1 to 7
e   day 8 to 14

f   day 15 to 21
g   day 22 to month's end
h   minor attainment
i   minor attainment
j   major attainment

212

```
        (g) 3                          (g) 5
        (f) 7                          (f) 9
    (d) 7   (e) 9                  (d) 8   (e) 1
(a) 5   (b) 2   (c) 7          (a) 6   (b) 2   (c) 8
    (h) 3   (i) 5                  (h) 4   (i) 6
        (j) 2                          (j) 2
         May                           June


        (g) 7                          (g) 9
        (f)11,9                        (f) 4
    (d) 9   (e) 11                 (d) 1   (e) 3
(a) 7   (b) 2   (c) 9          (a) 8   (b) 2   (c) 1
    (h) 5   (i) 7                  (h) 6   (i) 1
        (j) 2                          (j) 5
         July                         August
```

a	month digit	
b	personal year	
c	a + b	
d	day 1 to 7	
e	day 8 to 14	

f	day 15 to 21
g	day 22 to month's end
h	minor attainment
i	minor attainment
j	major attainment

            (g) 11,9
            (f) 22,2
        (d) 11   (e) 11,2
    (a) 9   (b) 2   (c) 11
        (h) 7   (i) 0
            (j) 7
        September

            (g) 4
            (f) 8
        (d) 3   (e) 5
    (a) 1   (b) 2   (c) 3
        (h) 1   (i) 1
            (j) 0
        October

            (g) 6
            (f) 1
        (d) 4   (e) 6
    (a) 2   (b) 2   (c) 4
        (h) 0   (i) 2
            (j) 2
        November

            (g) 8
            (f) 3
        (d) 5   (e) 7
    (a) 3   (b) 2   (c) 5
        (h) 1   (i) 3
            (j) 2
        December

a	month digit	f	day 15 to 21
b	personal year	g	day 22 to month's end
c	a + b	h	minor attainment
d	day 1 to 7	i	minor attainment
e	day 8 to 14	j	major attainment

Personal Year 3

	(g) 5	
	(f) 11	
(d) 4	(e) 7	
(a) 1	(b) 3	(c) 4
	(h) 2	(i) 1
	(j) 1	

January

	(g) 7	
	(f) 4	
(d) 5	(e) 8	
(a) 2	(b) 3	(c) 5
	(h) 1	(i) 2
	(j) 1	

February

	(g) 9	
	(f) 6	
(d) 6	(e) 9	
(a) 3	(b) 3	(c) 6
	(h) 0	(i) 3
	(j) 3	

March

	(g) 11	
	(f) 8	
(d) 7	(e) 1	
(a) 4	(b) 3	(c) 7
	(h) 1	(i) 4
	(j) 3	

April

a	month digit	f	day 15 to 21
b	personal year	g	day 22 to month's end
c	a + b	h	minor attainment
d	day 1 to 7	i	minor attainment
e	day 8 to 14	j	major attainment

(g) 4
────────
(f) 11,8
────────────
(d) 8   (e) 11
────────────────
(a) 5   (b) 3   (c) 8
────────────────────
(h) 2   (i) 5
────────────
(j) 3
────────
May

(g) 6
────────
(f) 3
────────────
(d) 9   (e) 3
────────────────
(a) 6   (b) 3   (c) 9
────────────────────
(h) 3   (i) 6
────────────
(j) 3
────────
June

(g) 8
────────
(f) 5
────────────
(d) 1   (e) 4
────────────────
(a) 7   (b) 3   (c) 1
────────────────────
(h) 4   (i) 2
────────────
(j) 2
────────
July

(g) 11,8
────────
(f) 22,3
────────────
(d) 11   (e) 11,3
────────────────
(a) 8   (b) 3   (c) 11
────────────────────
(h) 5   (i) 1
────────────
(j) 4
────────
August

a   month digit
b   personal year
c   a + b
d   day 1 to 7
e   day 8 to 14

f   day 15 to 21
g   day 22 to month's end
h   minor attainment
i   minor attainment
j   major attainment

$$\frac{\text{(g) 3}}{\text{(f) 9}}$$

(d) 3   (e) 6
(a) 9   (b) 3   (c) 3
(h) 6   (i) 0
(j) 6

September

$$\frac{\text{(g) 5}}{\text{(f) 11}}$$

(d) 4   (e) 7
(a) 1   (b) 3   (c) 4
(h) 2   (i) 1
(j) 1

October

$$\frac{\text{(g) 7}}{\text{(f) 4}}$$

(d) 5   (e) 8
(a) 2   (b) 3   (c) 5
(h) 1   (i) 2
(j) 1

November

$$\frac{\text{(g) 9}}{\text{(f) 6}}$$

(d) 6   (e) 9
(a) 3   (b) 3   (c) 6
(h) 0   (i) 3
(j) 3

December

a   month digit
b   personal year
c   a + b
d   day 1 to 7
e   day 8 to 14
f   day 15 to 21
g   day 22 to month's end
h   minor attainment
i   minor attainment
j   major attainment

Personal Year 4

	(g) 6	
	(f) 5	
(d) 5	(e) 9	
(a) 1	(b) 4	(c) 5
(h) 3	(i) 1	
	(j) 2	

January

	(g) 8	
	(f) 7	
(d) 6	(e) 1	
(a) 2	(b) 4	(c) 6
(h) 2	(i) 2	
	(j) 0	

February

	(g) 1	
	(f) 11,7	
(d) 7	(e) 11	
(a) 3	(b) 4	(c) 7
(h) 1	(i) 3	
	(j) 2	

March

	(g) 3	
	(f) 11	
(d) 8	(e) 3	
(a) 4	(b) 4	(c) 8
(h) 0	(i) 4	
	(j) 4	

April

a month digit
b personal year
c a + b
d day 1 to 7
e day 8 to 14
f day 15 to 21
g day 22 to month's end
h minor attainment
i minor attainment
j major attainment

218

```
                (g) 5
               ────────
                (f) 4
               ────────
          (d) 9    (e) 4
         ──────────────────
    (a) 5    (b) 4    (c) 9
   ────────────────────────────
         (h) 1    (i) 5
         ──────────────────
                (j) 4
               ────────
                May
```

```
                (g) 7
               ────────
                (f) 6
               ────────
          (d) 1    (e) 5
         ──────────────────
    (a) 6    (b) 4    (c) 1
   ────────────────────────────
         (h) 2    (i) 3
         ──────────────────
                (j) 1
               ────────
                June
```

```
                (g)11,7
               ─────────
                (f)22,4
               ─────────
          (d) 11   (e)11,4
         ──────────────────
    (a) 7    (b) 4    (c) 11
   ────────────────────────────
         (h) 3    (i) 2
         ──────────────────
                (j) 1
               ────────
                July
```

```
                (g) 11
               ────────
                (f) 1
               ────────
          (d) 3    (e) 7
         ──────────────────
    (a) 8    (b) 4    (c) 3
   ────────────────────────────
         (h) 4    (i) 1
         ──────────────────
                (j) 3
               ────────
                August
```

a   month digit
b   personal year
c   a + b
d   day 1 to 7
e   day 8 to 14

f   day 15 to 21
g   day 22 to month's end
h   minor attainment
i   minor attainment
j   major attainment

```
          (g) 4                          (g) 6
          (f) 3                          (f) 5
      (d) 4    (e) 8                  (d) 5    (e) 9
(a) 9   (b) 4   (c) 4          (a) 1   (b) 4   (c) 5
      (h) 5    (i) 0                  (h) 3    (i) 1
            (j) 5                          (j) 2
         September                        October
```

```
          (g) 8                          (g) 1
          (f) 7                          (f)11,7
      (d) 6    (e) 1                  (d) 7    (e) 11
(a) 2   (b) 4   (c) 6          (a) 3   (b) 4   (c) 7
      (h) 2    (i) 2                  (h) 1    (i) 3
            (j) 0                          (j) 2
         November                        December
```

a   month digit
b   personal year
c   a + b
d   day 1 to 7
e   day 8 to 14
f   day 15 to 21
g   day 22 to month's end
h   minor attainment
i   minor attainment
j   major attainment

Personal Year 5

(g) 7
(f) 11,6
(d) 6 (e) 11
(a) 1 (b) 5 (c) 6
(h) 4 (i) 1
(j) 3

January

(g) 9
(f) 1
(d) 7 (e) 3
(a) 2 (b) 5 (c) 7
(h) 3 (i) 2
(j) 1

February

(g) 11
(f) 3
(d) 8 (e) 4
(a) 3 (b) 5 (c) 8
(h) 2 (i) 3
(j) 1

March

(g) 4
(f) 5
(d) 9 (e) 5
(a) 4 (b) 5 (c) 9
(h) 1 (i) 4
(j) 3

April

a	month digit	f	day 15 to 21
b	personal year	g	day 22 to month's end
c	a + b	h	minor attainment
d	day 1 to 7	i	minor attainment
e	day 8 to 14	j	major attainment

(g) 6
(f) 7
(d) 1   (e) 6
(a) 5   (b) 5   (c) 1
(h) 0   (i) 4
(j) 4

May

(g) 11,6
(f) 22,5
(d) 11   (e) 11,5
(a) 6   (b) 5   (c) 11
(h) 1   (i) 3
(j) 2

June

(g) 1
(f) 11
(d) 3   (e) 8
(a) 7   (b) 5   (c) 3
(h) 2   (i) 2
(j) 0

July

(g) 3
(f) 4
(d) 4   (e) 9
(a) 8   (b) 5   (c) 4
(h) 3   (i) 1
(j) 2

August

a	month digit	f	day 15 to 21
b	personal year	g	day 22 to month's end
c	a + b	h	minor attainment
d	day 1 to 7	i	minor attainment
e	day 8 to 14	j	major attainment

	(g) 5	
	(f) 6	
	(d) 5	(e) 1
(a) 9	(b) 5	(c) 5
	(h) 4	(i) 0
	(j) 4	

September

	(g) 7	
	(f) 11,6	
	(d) 6	(e) 11
(a) 1	(b) 5	(c) 6
	(h) 4	(i) 1
	(j) 3	

October

	(g) 9	
	(f) 1	
	(d) 7	(e) 3
(a) 2	(b) 5	(c) 7
	(h) 3	(i) 2
	(j) 1	

November

	(g) 11	
	(f) 3	
	(d) 8	(e) 4
(a) 3	(b) 5	(c) 8
	(h) 2	(i) 3
	(j) 1	

December

a month digit
b personal year
c a + b
d day 1 to 7
e day 8 to 14
f day 15 to 21
g day 22 to month's end
h minor attainment
i minor attainment
j major attainment

Personal Year 6

(g) 8

(f) 11

(d) 7   (e) 4

(a) 1   (b) 6   (c) 7

(h) 5   (i) 1

(j) 4

January

(g) 1

(f) 4

(d) 8   (e) 5

(a) 2   (b) 6   (c) 8

(h) 4   (i) 2

(j) 2

February

(g) 3

(f) 6

(d) 9   (e) 6

(a) 3   (b) 6   (c) 9

(h) 3   (i) 3

(j) 0

March

(g) 5

(f) 8

(d) 1   (e) 7

(a) 4   (b) 6   (c) 1

(h) 2   (i) 5

(j) 3

April

a   month digit
b   personal year
c   a + b
d   day 1 to 7
e   day 8 to 14
f   day 15 to 21
g   day 22 to month's end
h   minor attainment
i   minor attainment
j   major attainment

224

```
        (g)11,5                       (g) 9
        (f)22,6                       (f) 3
    (d) 11  (e)11,6               (d) 3   (e) 9
(a) 5   (b) 6   (c) 11       (a) 6   (b) 6   (c) 3
    (h) 1   (i) 4                 (h) 0   (i) 3
        (j) 3                         (j) 3
         May                          June
```

```
        (g) 11                        (g) 4
        (f) 5                         (f)11,5
    (d) 4   (e) 1                 (d) 5   (e) 11
(a) 7   (b) 6   (c) 4         (a) 8   (b) 6   (c) 5
    (h) 1   (i) 2                 (h) 2   (i) 1
        (j) 1                         (j) 1
         July                        August
```

a	month digit	f	day 15 to 21
b	personal year	g	day 22 to month's end
c	a + b	h	minor attainment
d	day 1 to 7	i	minor attainment
e	day 8 to 14	j	major attainment

	(g) 6	
	(f) 9	
(d) 6		(e) 3
(a) 9	(b) 6	(c) 6
(h) 3		(i) 0
	(j) 3	

September

	(g) 8	
	(f) 11	
(d) 7		(e) 4
(a) 1	(b) 6	(c) 7
(h) 5		(i) 1
	(j) 4	

October

	(g) 1	
	(f) 4	
(d) 8		(e) 5
(a) 2	(b) 6	(c) 8
(h) 4		(i) 2
	(j) 2	

November

	(g) 3	
	(f) 6	
(d) 9		(e) 6
(a) 3	(b) 6	(c) 9
(h) 3		(i) 3
	(j) 0	

December

a	month digit	f	day 15 to 21
b	personal year	g	day 22 to month's end
c	a + b	h	minor attainment
d	day 1 to 7	i	minor attainment
e	day 8 to 14	j	major attainment

Personal Year 7

	(g) 9	
	(f) 5	
(d) 8	(e) 6	
(a) 1	(b) 7	(c) 8
(h) 6	(i) 1	
	(j) 5	

January

	(g) 11	
	(f) 7	
(d) 9	(e) 7	
(a) 2	(b) 7	(c) 9
(h) 5	(i) 2	
	(j) 3	

February

	(g) 4	
	(f) 9	
(d) 1	(e) 8	
(a) 3	(b) 7	(c) 1
(h) 4	(i) 6	
	(j) 2	

March

	(g) 11,4	
	(f) 22,7	
(d) 11	(e) 11,7	
(a) 4	(b) 7	(c) 11
(h) 3	(i) 5	
	(j) 2	

April

a month digit	f day 15 to 21
b personal year	g day 22 to month's end
c a + b	h minor attainment
d day 1 to 7	i minor attainment
e day 8 to 14	j major attainment

```
        (g) 8                           (g) 1
        (f) 4                           (f)11,4
    (d) 3    (e) 1                   (d) 4    (e) 11
(a) 5   (b) 7   (c) 3            (a) 6   (b) 7   (c) 4
    (h) 2    (i) 4                   (h) 1    (i) 3
        (j) 2                           (j) 2
        May                             June


        (g) 3                           (g) 5
        (f) 8                           (f) 1
    (d) 5    (e) 3                   (d) 6    (e) 4
(a) 7   (b) 7   (c) 5            (a) 8   (b) 7   (c) 6
    (h) 0    (i) 2                   (h) 1    (i) 1
        (j) 2                           (j) 0
        July                            August
```

a   month digit
b   personal year
c   a + b
d   day 1 to 7
e   day 8 to 14

f   day 15 to 21
g   day 22 to month's end
h   minor attainment
i   minor attainment
j   major attainment

228

```
        (g) 7
       ─────────
        (f) 3
       ─────────
    (d) 7   (e) 5
   ──────────────────
(a) 9   (b) 7   (c) 7
   ──────────────────
    (h) 2   (i) 0
       ─────────
        (j) 2
       ─────────
      September
```

```
        (g) 9
       ─────────
        (f) 5
       ─────────
    (d) 8   (e) 6
   ──────────────────
(a) 1   (b) 7   (c) 8
   ──────────────────
    (h) 6   (i) 1
       ─────────
        (j) 5
       ─────────
        October
```

```
        (g) 11
       ─────────
        (f) 7
       ─────────
    (d) 9   (e) 7
   ──────────────────
(a) 2   (b) 7   (c) 9
   ──────────────────
    (h) 5   (i) 2
       ─────────
        (j) 3
       ─────────
       November
```

```
        (g) 4
       ─────────
        (f) 9
       ─────────
    (d) 1   (e) 8
   ──────────────────
(a) 3   (b) 7   (c) 1
   ──────────────────
    (h) 4   (i) 6
       ─────────
        (j) 2
       ─────────
       December
```

a	month digit	f	day 15 to 21
b	personal year	g	day 22 to month's end
c	a + b	h	minor attainment
d	day 1 to 7	i	minor attainment
e	day 8 to 14	j	major attainment

Personal Year 8

	(g) 1	
	(f) 8	
	(d) 9 (e) 8	
(a) 1	(b) 8	(c) 9
	(h) 7 (i) 1	
	(j) 6	

January

	(g) 3	
	(f) 1	
	(d) 1 (e) 9	
(a) 2	(b) 8	(c) 1
	(h) 6 (i) 7	
	(j) 1	

February

	(g) 11,3	
	(f) 22,8	
	(d) 11 (e) 11,8	
(a) 3	(b) 8	(c) 11
	(h) 5 (i) 6	
	(j) 1	

March

	(g) 7	
	(f) 11,3	
	(d) 3 (e) 11	
(a) 4	(b) 8	(c) 3
	(h) 4 (i) 5	
	(j) 1	

April

a month digit	f day 15 to 21
b personal year	g day 22 to month's end
c a + b	h minor attainment
d day 1 to 7	i minor attainment
e day 8 to 14	j major attainment

230

```
        (g) 9
        (f) 7
   (d) 4   (e) 3
(a) 5  (b) 8  (c) 4
   (h) 3   (i) 4
        (j) 1
         May
```

```
        (g) 11
        (f) 9
   (d) 5   (e) 4
(a) 6  (b) 8  (c) 5
   (h) 2   (i) 3
        (j) 1
         June
```

```
        (g) 4
        (f) 11
   (d) 6   (e) 5
(a) 7  (b) 8  (c) 6
   (h) 1   (i) 2
        (j) 1
         July
```

```
        (g) 6
        (f) 4
   (d) 7   (e) 6
(a) 8  (b) 8  (c) 7
   (h) 0   (i) 1
        (j) 1
        August
```

a	month digit	
b	personal year	
c	a + b	
d	day 1 to 7	
e	day 8 to 14	

f	day 15 to 21	
g	day 22 to month's end	
h	minor attainment	
i	minor attainment	
j	major attainment	

231

(g) 8
(f) 6
(d) 8   (e) 7
(a) 9   (b) 8   (c) 8
(h) 1   (i) 0
(j) 1
September

(g) 1
(f) 8
(d) 9   (e) 8
(a) 1   (b) 8   (c) 9
(h) 7   (i) 1
(j) 6
October

(g) 3
(f) 1
(d) 1   (e) 9
(a) 2   (b) 8   (c) 1
(h) 6   (i) 7
(j) 1
November

(g)11,3
(f)22,8
(d) 11 (e)11,8
(a) 3   (b) 8   (c) 11
(h) 5   (i) 6
(j) 1
December

a   month digit
b   personal year
c   a + b
d   day 1 to 7
e   day 8 to 14

f   day 15 to 21
g   day 22 to month's end
h   minor attainment
i   minor attainment
j   major attainment

Personal Year 9

```
        (g) 2
        ─────
        (f) 2
        ─────
    (d) 1   (e) 1
    ─────   ─────
(a) 1   (b) 9   (c) 1
    ─────   ─────
    (h) 8   (i) 8
        ─────
        (j) 0
        ─────
      January
```

```
        (g)11,2
        ──────
        (f)22,9
        ──────
    (d) 11  (e)11,9
    ──────  ──────
(a) 2   (b) 9   (c) 11
    ─────   ──────
    (h) 7   (i) 7
        ─────
        (j) 0
        ─────
      February
```

```
        (g) 6
        ─────
        (f) 6
        ─────
    (d) 3   (e) 3
    ─────   ─────
(a) 3   (b) 9   (c) 3
    ─────   ─────
    (h) 6   (i) 6
        ─────
        (j) 0
        ─────
       March
```

```
        (g) 8
        ─────
        (f) 8
        ─────
    (d) 4   (e) 4
    ─────   ─────
(a) 4   (b) 9   (c) 4
    ─────   ─────
    (h) 5   (i) 5
        ─────
        (j) 0
        ─────
       April
```

a   month digit
b   personal year
c   a + b
d   day 1 to 7
e   day 8 to 14
f   day 15 to 21
g   day 22 to month's end
h   minor attainment
i   minor attainment
j   major attainment

```
          (g) 1
         ─────────
          (f) 1
         ─────────
     (d) 5    (e) 5
    ─────────────────
 (a) 5   (b) 9   (c) 5
    ─────────────────
     (h) 4    (i) 4
         ─────────
          (j) 0
         ─────────
           May
```

```
          (g) 3
         ─────────
          (f) 3
         ─────────
     (d) 6    (e) 6
    ─────────────────
 (a) 6   (b) 9   (c) 6
    ─────────────────
     (h) 3    (i) 3
         ─────────
          (j) 0
         ─────────
           June
```

```
          (g) 5
         ─────────
          (f) 5
         ─────────
     (d) 7    (e) 7
    ─────────────────
 (a) 7   (b) 9   (c) 7
    ─────────────────
     (h) 2    (i) 2
         ─────────
          (j) 0
         ─────────
           July
```

```
          (g) 7
         ─────────
          (f) 7
         ─────────
     (d) 8    (e) 8
    ─────────────────
 (a) 8   (b) 9   (c) 8
    ─────────────────
     (h) 1    (i) 1
         ─────────
          (j) 0
         ─────────
          August
```

a	month digit	f	day 15 to 21
b	personal year	g	day 22 to month's end
c	a + b	h	minor attainment
d	day 1 to 7	i	minor attainment
e	day 8 to 14	j	major attainment

(g) 9

(f) 9

(d) 9   (e) 9

(a) 9   (b) 9   (c) 9

(h) 0   (i) 0

(j) 0

September

(g) 2

(f) 2

(d) 1   (e) 1

(a) 1   (b) 9   (c) 1

(h) 8   (i) 8

(j) 0

October

(g) 11,2

(f) 22,9

(d) 11   (e) 11,9

(a) 2   (b) 9   (c) 11

(h) 7   (i) 7

(j) 0

November

(g) 6

(f) 6

(d) 3   (e) 3

(a) 3   (b) 9   (c) 3

(h) 6   (i) 6

(j) 0

December

a	month digit	
b	personal year	
c	a + b	
d	day 1 to 7	
e	day 8 to 14	
f	day 15 to 21	
g	day 22 to month's end	
h	minor attainment	
i	minor attainment	
j	major attainment	

Personal Year 11

(g)11,2
(f)33,2
(d)11,1 (e)22,1
(a) 1 (b) 11 (c)11,1
(h) 1 (i) 1
(j) 0
January

(g)11,4
(f)33,4
(d)11,2 (e)22,2
(a) 2 (b) 11 (c)11,2
(h) 0 (i) 2
(j) 2
February

(g)11,6
(f)33,6
(d)11,3 (e)22,3
(a) 3 (b) 11 (c)11,3
(h) 1 (i) 3
(j) 2
March

(g)11,8
(f)33,8
(d)11,4 (e)22,4
(a) 4 (b) 11 (c)11,4
(h) 2 (i) 4
(j) 2
April

a   month digit
b   personal year
c   a + b
d   day 1 to 7
e   day 8 to 14
f   day 15 to 21
g   day 22 to month's end
h   minor attainment
i   minor attainment
j   major attainment

(g)11,1
(f)33,1
(d)11,5 (e)22,5
(a) 5   (b) 11 (c)11,5
(h) 3   (i) 5
(j) 2
May

(g)11,3
(f)33,3
(d)11,6 (e)22,6
(a) 6   (b) 11 (c)11,6
(h) 4   (i) 6
(j) 2
June

(g)11,5
(f)33,5
(d)11,7 (e)22,7
(a) 7   (b) 11 (c)11,7
(h) 5   (i) 7
(j) 2
July

(g)11,7
(f)33,7
(d)11,8 (e)22,8
(a) 8   (b) 11 (c)11,8
(h) 6   (i) 1
(j) 5
August

a	month digit	
b	personal year	
c	a + b	
d	day 1 to 7	
e	day 8 to 14	
f	day 15 to 21	
g	day 22 to month's end	
h	minor attainment	
i	minor attainment	
j	major attainment	

(g)11,9
(f)33,9
(d)11,9 (e)22,9
(a) 9 (b) 11 (c)11,9
(h) 7 (i) 0
(j) 7

September

(g)11,2
(f)33,2
(d)11,1 (e)22,1
(a) 1 (b) 11 (c)11,1
(h) 1 (i) 1
(j) 0

October

(g)11,4
(f)33,4
(d)11,2 (e)22,2
(a) 2 (b) 11 (c)11,2
(h) 0 (i) 2
(j) 2

November

(g)11,6
(f)33,6
(d)11,3 (e)22,3
(a) 3 (b) 11 (c)11,3
(h) 1 (i) 3
(j) 2

December

a	month digit	
b	personal year	
c	a + b	
d	day 1 to 7	
e	day 8 to 14	
f	day 15 to 21	
g	day 22 to month's end	
h	minor attainment	
i	minor attainment	
j	major attainment	

Personal Year 22

(g)22,2
(f)66,2
(d)22,1 (e)44,1
(a) 1 (b) 22 (c)22,1
(h) 3 (i) 1
(j) 2

January

(g)22,4
(f)66,4
(d)22,2 (e)44,2
(a) 2 (b) 22 (c)22,2
(h) 2 (i) 2
(j) 0

February

(g)22,6
(f)66,6
(d)22,3 (e)44,3
(a) 3 (b) 22 (c)22,3
(h) 1 (i) 3
(j) 2

March

(g)22,8
(f)66,8
(d)22,4 (e)44,4
(a) 4 (b) 22 (c)22,4
(h) 0 (i) 4
(j) 4

April

a	month digit	f day 15 to 21
b	personal year	g day 22 to month's end
c	a + b	h minor attainment
d	day 1 to 7	i minor attainment
e	day 8 to 14	j major attainment

(g)22,1

(f)66,1

(d)22,5 (e)44,5

(a) 5 (b) 22 (c)22,5

(h) 1 (i) 5

(j) 4

May

(g)22,3

(f)66,3

(d)22,6 (e)44,6

(a) 6 (b) 22 (c)22,6

(h) 2 (i) 3

(j) 1

June

(g)22,5

(f)66,5

(d)22,7 (e)44,7

(a) 7 (b) 22 (c)22,7

(h) 3 (i) 2

(j) 1

July

(g)22,7

(f)66,7

(d)22,8 (e)44,8

(a) 8 (b) 22 (c)22,8

(h) 4 (i) 1

(j) 3

August

a	month digit	
b	personal year	
c	a + b	
d	day 1 to 7	
e	day 8 to 14	

f	day 15 to 21	
g	day 22 to month's end	
h	minor attainment	
i	minor attainment	
j	major attainment	

240

$$(g)22,9$$
$$(f)66,9$$
$$(d)22,9 \quad (e)44,9$$
$$(a)\ 9 \quad (b)\ 22 \quad (c)22,9$$
$$(h)\ 5 \quad (i)\ 0$$
$$(j)\ 5$$

September

$$(g)22,2$$
$$(f)66,2$$
$$(d)22,1 \quad (e)44,1$$
$$(a)\ 1 \quad (b)\ 22 \quad (c)22,1$$
$$(h)\ 3 \quad (i)\ 1$$
$$(j)\ 2$$

October

$$(g)22,4$$
$$(f)66,4$$
$$(d)22,2 \quad (e)44,2$$
$$(a)\ 2 \quad (b)\ 22 \quad (c)22,2$$
$$(h)\ 2 \quad (i)\ 2$$
$$(j)\ 0$$

November

$$(g)22,6$$
$$(f)66,6$$
$$(d)22,3 \quad (e)44,3$$
$$(a)\ 3 \quad (b)\ 22 \quad (c)22,3$$
$$(h)\ 1 \quad (i)\ 3$$
$$(j)\ 2$$

December

a   month digit
b   personal year
c   a + b
d   day 1 to 7
e   day 8 to 14
f   day 15 to 21
g   day 22 to month's end
h   minor attainment
i   minor attainment
j   major attainment

November as an 11

| (g)22,1 |
| (f)22,3 |

(d)11,1 (e)11,2

(a) 11   (b) 1   (c)11,1

(h) 1   (i) 2

(j) 1

Personal Year 1

| (g)22,2 |
| (f)22,6 |

(d)11,2 (e)11,4

(a) 11   (b) 2   (c)11,2

(h) 0   (i) 2

(j) 2

Personal Year 2

| (g)22,3 |
| (f)22,9 |

(d)11,3 (e)11,6

(a) 11   (b) 3   (c)11,3

(h) 1   (i) 2

(j) 1

Personal Year 3

| (g)22,4 |
| (f)22,3 |

(d)11,4 (e)11,8

(a) 11   (b) 4   (c)11,4

(h) 2   (i) 2

(j) 0

Personal Year 4

a	month digit	f	day 15 to 21
b	personal year	g	day 22 to month's end
c	a + b	h	minor attainment
d	day 1 to 7	i	minor attainment
e	day 8 to 14	j	major attainment

242

	(g)22,5	
	(f)22,6	
(d)11,5		(e)11,1
(a) 11	(b) 5	(c)11,5
(h) 3		(i) 2
	(j) 1	

Personal Year 5

	(g)22,6	
	(f)22,9	
(d)11,6		(e)11,3
(a) 11	(b) 6	(c)11,6
(h) 4		(i) 2
	(j) 2	

Personal Year 6

	(g)22,7	
	(f)22,3	
(d)11,7		(e)11,5
(a) 11	(b) 7	(c)11,7
(h) 5		(i) 2
	(j) 3	

Personal Year 7

	(g)22,8	
	(f)22,6	
(d)11,8		(e)11,7
(a) 11	(b) 8	(c)11,8
(h) 6		(i) 7
	(j) 1	

Personal Year 8

a   month digit
b   personal year
c   a + b
d   day 1 to 7
e   day 8 to 14

f   day 15 to 21
g   day 22 to month's end
h   minor attainment
i   minor attainment
j   major attainment

(g)22,9
(f)22,9
(d)11,9　(e)11,9
(a) 11　(b) 9　(c)11,9
(h) 7　(i) 7
(j) 0

Personal Year 9

(g) 33
(f) 55
(d) 22　(e) 33
(a) 11　(b) 11　(c) 22
(h) 0　(i) 2
(j) 2

Personal Year 11

(g) 44
(f) 88
(d) 33　(e) 55
(a) 11　(b) 22　(c) 33
(h) 2　(i) 2
(j) 0

Personal Year 22

a month digit	f day 15 to 21
b personal year	g day 22 to month's end
c a + b	h minor attainment
d day 1 to 7	i minor attainment
e day 8 to 14	j major attainment

Glossary

Attainment

What can be attained or obtained during the month is called the attainment. In the numerology chart for assessing times to seek compatibility, the attainment is the bottom triangle.

The term "attainment" is first found in chapter 6.

Compound Numbers

When a main nine number and a master number are combined, or a master number and a master number are combined, what is formed is called a compound number. Compound numbers are written with a comma between the parts of the number. Compound numbers are formed because master numbers are not reduced. Examples of compound numbers are: (11,3), (11,8), (22,1), (33,4) or (44,2). *The term "compound number" is first found in Chapter 1.*

Day Digit

The day digit is the numerology equivalent of the number of a day. It has to be reduced as far as possible. The day digit may be one of the main nine numbers or a master number. *The term "day digit" is first found in Chapter 6.*

Descriptor Numbers

Descriptor numbers are numbers that are not for finding compatibility by themselves, but can help describe a good number for compatibility. Descriptor numbers are 1, 4, 7, 8, and 44. Descriptor numbers can be simple numbers or part of a compound number. *The term "descriptor number" is first found in Chapter 6.*

The Expression Number

The expression number is the sum of the total name. This number shows a person's overall personality. To find the expression number, use the whole name as it appears on the birth certificate. In the case of adoption, use the name given at birth if it is known. The original name will have the strongest vibrations. A name change, such as in adoption, will give some change of vibration, but the strongest vibrations will still be with the original name. In the case of a name having Sr. or Jr. following it, find the expression number both with and without Sr. or Jr.. The Sr. or Jr. may or may not influence the vibrations. *The term "expression number" is first found in Chapter 1.*

Inner Self

The inner self is the part of the personality that the world sees. It is determined by finding the numerology sum of the consonants in the name. There are other names for the inner self. It is sometimes called the quiet self or the latent self. The inner self is thought to be a part of the personality that is used to try to obtain the soul urge.

The term "inner self" is first found in Chapter 3.

Inner Structure

The inner structure is composed of the soul urge and the inner self. It is formed from the vowels and consonants of the name.

The term "inner structure" is first found in Chapter 3.

Lower Vibration

The lower vibration is the equivalent of a master number when it is reduced. Examples of this are as follows. The lower vibration of 11 is 2. The lower vibration of 22 is 4. The lower vibration of 33 is 6.

The term "lower vibration" is first found in Chapter 1.

Main Nine Numbers

The numbers 1 through 9 are the main nine numbers. The main nine numbers are the basic building blocks of numerology.

The term "main nine number" is first found in Chapter 1.

Master Numbers

Master numbers are the numbers made up of the same two digits, such as 11, 22, 33 and 44. These numbers are thought to be stronger or more charged with energy than the main nine numbers. In addition, master numbers are not reduced.

The term "master number" is first found in Chapter 1.

Month Digit

The numerology number for a given month is called the month digit. It is reduced as far as possible. The following table shows the month digits. The month of November is the only one that is different, as it has two possibilities. The 11 of the number for November can be either an 11 or a 2. Try to tell if the person is living as a 2 or as an 11 before choosing whether to use the master number or its lower vibration.

January	1	February	2
March	3	April	4
May	5	June	6
July	7	August	8
September	9	October	$10 = (1+0) = 1$
November	$11 = (1+1) = 2$ or 11		
December	$12 = (1+2) = 3$		

The term "month digit" is first found in Chapter 6.

Personal Year

The numerology number for how a year will affect an individual personally is called the personal year. The personal year is found by finding the universal year and then adding it to the month and day of birth. The month and day of birth should first be reduced as far as possible.

The term "personal year" is found in Chapter 6.

Simple Numbers

Simple numbers are the main nine numbers as they stand alone, or the master numbers as they stand alone. They are numbers that are not in the compound form.

The term "simple numbers" is found in Chapter 1.

Soul Urge

The soul urge is the sum of the vowels of a name. The soul urge is what motivates a person or what a person seeks within his or her heart. It is the person's heart's desire.

In reading about numerology, the name numerologists give to this number may change. Some call it the soul urge, some the heart's desire, and other call it the secret ambition. Whatever term is used, the meaning and evaluation of this number is the same.

The term "soul urge" is first found in Chapter 3.

Universal Year

The universal year is the numerology number for a particular year. It is always the same for everyone. The universal year is found by adding the digits of a year and then reducing them down as far as they can be reduced in numerology terms. The following list will show the universal year for several years.

2009 = 2+0+0+9 = 11
2023 = 2+0+2+3 = 7
2035 = 2+0+3+5 = 10 = 1 + 0 = 1

The term "universal year" is first found in Chapter 6.

Vowels

The vowels used in numerology are: a, e, i, o, u and some-times y, as in regular usage in the English language. If there is no other vowel in the syllable, then use y as the vowel. *The definition for vowels is first found in Chapter 3.*

Week Digit

The week digit is the numerology number for the vibration of a specific week. It may be one of the main nine num-bers, a master number, or a compound number.

Week digits vary. To find the week digit of the first 7 days of the month, add the month digit and the personal year in the numerology chart for looking for compatibili-ty. This is position a and b added. To find the second week (the 8th to the 14th), add the personal year and third num-ber in the base line of the numerology chart. This is posi-tion b and c. To find the third week (the 15th to the 21st, including the 21st), add the week digits for week 1 and week 2. This is position d and e added together, which equals position f. To find the last part of the month, which is usually longer than a week (the 22nd to the end of the month), add the month digit and the third number in the base line. This is position a and position c.

The term "week digit" is first found in Chapter 6.